A
GUIDE
FOR THE
PARENTS
OF
HORSE-CRAZY KIDS

A
GUIDE
FOR THE
PARENTS
OF
HORSE-CRAZY KIDS

Frances Wilbur

Foreword by Hilda Gurney

Half Halt Press
Middletown, Maryland

A Guide for the Parents of Horse-Crazy Kids
© 1990 Frances P. Wilbur
Illustrations © 1990 Lyn Lyons

Published in the United States of America by
Half Halt Press, Inc.
6416 Burkittsville Road
Middletown, MD 21769

Cover and text design by Clara Graves
Typesetting and layout by Rebecca Hocker

Library of Congress Cataloging-in-Publication Data

Wilbur, Frances.
    A guide for the parents of horse-crazy kids / Frances Wilbur.
        p.   cm.
    Includes bibliographical references (p.) and index.
    ISBN 0-939481-20-0 : $16.95
    1. Horses.
SF285.W65   1990
636.1--dc20   90-5116
                                                                    CIP

To my loving husband Bill

Acknowledgments

To be honest about acknowledgments for this book, I would have to name all the teachers and horses I've ever known. But there are special people who have helped me with the preparation of this manuscript, and those I wish to thank in print as well as in person.

Nancy Evans, for her time and expertise in editing and also her enthusiasm and inspiration, Roger Ott for taking time out from his cutting horses to read and make comment, Stephanie Abronson and Wendy West for their research and contributions, Lyn Lyons for her drawings, Karen Hendricks for her camera work, Don Burch who kept the computer going in spite of power failures, Harry Hoffman who made the software work for me, Joe Dendy DVM, Vince Jessup DVM, and John Tolley, DVM, for their contributions in technical knowledge, Billy and Roberta Robertson for their expert opinions, my family for their help and understanding, and most of all my husband, Bill, whose loving support and encouragement made this task a happy one.

I would especially like to thank those who contributed photographs: Stephanie Abronson, Pony Cross Farm, Calabasas, CA pp. 19, 113, 157, 190; American Vaulting Association p. 90 (photo by Cindy Paul); Colorado Kiwi Co., Clark, CO p. 108; Carol Cusimano p. 161 (photo by Mary Dukes); Carol Dzindzio, Twin Oaks Valley Morgans, p. 164; Joan Ervin, Merry-Go-Round-Manor Connemaras, Morgan Hill, CA p. 116; Nancy Evans, p. 16; Karen Hendricks, Bakersfield, CA jacket portrait and pp. 25, 26, 78, 138, 153, 169; Anne Kirkpatrick pp. 21, 49; Lawrence Brothers Inc., Sterling, IL p. 108; Laurie McNally, cover photo; Roger Ott's Cutting Horses, Bakersfield, CA p. 152; Pony of the Americas Club, Inc. pp. 17, 59, 99; Don Reiman, Inglenook Farm Morgans, p. 115; Ring-O-Steel Corp., Torrance, CA pp. 105, 106; Kim Sawyer p. 160; Marie Schell p. 112; Joan Webster, Stoneybrook Connemaras, Napa, CA pp. 156, 158, 191; Georgia Wiester, pp. 159, 163 (photo by Ed Lawrence); and Anne Kirkpatrick, p. 199.

Contents

Your child's fascination. . . .part of growing up. . . .horses are not for everybody. . . .the duration of the craze. . . .who's going to stay with it. . . .why more girls than boys. . . .positive addiction.

The gap between the dream and the reality. . . .learn first and buy later. . . .two types of riding. . . .Western and English, saddles and sports. . . .safe ways of bridging the gap: 4-H Clubs; U.S. Pony Clubs. . . .if none are available.

No teaching requirements. . . .the ideal teacher. . . .5 kinds of stables: riding clubs, riding schools and academies, training stables, boarding stables, rental stables.

What to look for at stables. . . .weekly lessons. . . .summer programs. . . .day camps. . . .resident camps. . . .accredited school programs.

....*activities....insurance....why you shouldn't buy a horse....alternatives—books, work, vaulting.*

Chapter 21 **Four Feet On The Ground** 187

Don't compromise quality for feed, farrier, and first aid....you can economize with vet clinics....fitting and taking care of tack properly....riding clinics, local horse shows, do-it-yourself sports....leave trailering to experts....definition of stable personnel.

Chapter 22 **Eyes On The Horizon** 195

Importance of parent power....the right kind of help.... parents being taken advantage of....the value of an object.... never forget to have fun....success and excellence are not the same....few can have success, but excellence is open to all.... persistence and determination are omnipotent....Pegasus is a symbol.

Foreword

I recommend this book highly for any one interested in learning about and understanding horses, especially those parents whose children are starting to ride. Frances Wilbur, in a light, entertaining and authoritative manner explains how the horse works and the best approach to learning about horses and riding.

The author has had years of experience in riding and in directing a children's riding camp at their ranch in the beautiful Southern Sierras of California as well as in hosting Combined Training events. She shows thorough understanding of the relationship of children, parents, and horses. The author draws on events from her long experience to illustrate the basic nature of horses.

From my viewpoint as a dedicated rider and instructor, this book fills a void for parents and friends of young riders as well as helping horse persons to understand their beloved equines more fully.

Hilda Gurney
Bronze Medal, Olympic Games, 1976
Gold Medal, Pan American Games, 1975
and 1979
Silver Medal, Pan American Games, 1983
Winner, six times, National Grand Prix
Dressage Championship, 1975, 1976,
1977, 1979, 1984 and 1985

Introduction

All during the years I was teaching riding and horsemanship to children, I longed for a book I could put in the hands of the parents and say, "Here, read this. Then you will have a better idea of why I am teaching your youngsters these things, why your children are having those problems, why you should appreciate what they are doing more than you do, and what you can do to *really* help."

I wanted a book I could give to the parents who knew nothing about horses and hadn't the foggiest notion of how to cope with a horse-crazy youngster, a book which would provide them with help *before* they got involved with horses; a book which would save them time, effort, money, and grief.

Not all persons should have children, and not all persons should have horses. I wanted a book which would give every parent a basis on which to make a sound judgment about horse ownership. For those who decided not to have horses, I wanted them to be able to say no to their youngsters without feeling guilty.

And for those who would eventually thrive on having a horse, I wanted a book that would point them in the right direction with the least trauma.

There are excellent books on learning how to ride and on buying and taking care of a horse, but all are addressed to the person who loves horses and who is hoping to buy one. There's a vast difference between embarking with enthusiasm toward your own goal, and approaching reluctantly what may be a scarey adventure for the sake of your youngster. There was no book addressed to the non-horse-person parent, so I wrote one.

This book is for all those grown-ups who are willing to explore an unknown world because they are conscientious and want to make decisions that are best for their youngsters. It's for all those grown-ups who thought they knew what they were doing when they bought a horse, and now feel that they are dealing with an alien from another planet in their own back yard. It's for all those grown-ups who are beginning to sense the magnetism that horses have for human beings.

If you are an adult who is being driven up the wall by a youngster who wants a horse, this book is for you.

Chapter 1

You Are Not Alone

*Your child's fascination....part of growing up....
horses are not for everybody....the duration of the
craze....who's going to stay with it....why more girls
than boys....positive addiction.*

For the past two or three years your youngster has been fascinated by horses. Lately the interest has accelerated. Now you have to admit it — your child is crazy over horses. Where in the world, you ask yourself, did this attachment come from?

Maybe you have forgotten that you were horse-crazy at that age. Or perhaps when you were growing up, no one in your family had the slightest interest in equines. If anyone did, that interest was quickly dispelled by an unfortunate incident. It might have been a quiet trail horse that spooked at an invisible object and rocketed all the way back to the barn with his terrified rider. Or a plodding four-legged giant grimly determined to go his own way, regardless of the kicks and tugs of the child on his back. Or a gentle pony that suddenly became a brat, took off bucking, and dumped his rider in the muck. An occurrence like this is enough to disillusion any would-be horseman.

Or perhaps you were never interested at all. Some people don't like mountain climbing, and there are those to whom hang-gliding has no appeal. You happen not to like horses. Or you like them — from a distance. But your daughter's bookshelves are bulging with horse stories. From your son's bedroom walls, horses leap at you on posters. In either child's room, plastic and ceramic models of horses graze, trot, and gallop over every inch of dresser space. At the dinner table the conversation always gets around to horses, even when you are determined that it will not.

You might vaguely remember having a "crush" like this when you were young, on a different subject, and you wait for the passion to run its course. Unfortunately, it doesn't. You are beginning to find clippings from the classified ads, Horses, Sale of, posted on the refrigerator door, propped on the dresser, or stuck in the bathroom mirror. With growing horror you realize that this passion may not be just a passing fancy. Suppose your child is *serious* about horses? You are a conscientious parent. If your child's dedication is genuine, you want to do something about it, but what? Where do you start?

Megan was seven in this photo when she rode her Shetland/Welsh pony Goblin in her first Pony Club Rally. She still loves horses. Very shortly she will be a licensed veterinarian and plans to specialize in equine research.

A parent who grew up in a horse-oriented family or who spent his childhood in the country with horses may have a good idea of what to do next — a fairly good idea. Let's see, how many years has it been since you had a horse? Never mind, right now you are not a horse person, and a little refresher course would come in handy. Besides, it's possible some things have changed.

Or suppose you never were a horse person. You might even have terrifying visions of an enormous, aggressive, and very strong animal who knows that you are afraid and is determined to take advantage of it.

You feel the order of your homelife threatened; your security slipping away. You want to climb onto the rooftop and yell "HELP!" at the top of your lungs.

Take heart! You are not alone, and help is at hand. This book is for you, the non-horse person with the horse-crazy kid.

Horses are not for everybody. For those who do enjoy horses, they can be a source of pleasure, a stimulating challenge, and excellent therapy in times of emotional stress.

Other people, and you may be among them, are completely turned off by horses. However, you probably have a child. At least one child, or you might not be reading this book. It may comfort you to know that in many ways, horses are just like young children. If you have been able to get along with your child, you will be able to get along with a horse. Having your child involved with horses does not have to be a disaster for you or for your family.

Being horse-crazy occurs so frequently among ten-to-twelve-year-olds that it might be considered a normal phase of growing up. Experience at our summer horsemanship camp over many years has shown that the horse-crazy stage is likely to last from two to four years. The peak years are ages ten to fourteen.

A few youngsters devoted to riding find that when they enter high school, the time they spend with horses is gradually taken over by homework and school-related activities. Yet there are some who manage

Allen is seven and his best buddy is his six-year-old POA pony, Freckles.

17

to keep up their riding all through high school. If they had begun earlier than age ten, this means a duration of about eight years. Some give up riding through necessity when they go away to college. Others continue riding until they get married and start having children. Then there are those who never outgrow this dedication. Horses are part of our lives.

An interesting sequel to the earlier horse interest is the number of adults who, after their children are grown, go back to horseback riding and have even more fun than they did before.

You can't help but wonder how long your child will be interested in horses, and what your child will think of next. You want to know how much of an investment to make. Suppose you go all out for horses, and the next week your son is discovered by the school track coach? Or your daughter discovers boys? Will all your time and effort be wasted? How can you tell?

Your child's own nature will give you some clues as to how long this passion may last. Does your child love and enjoy caring for animals? If you bought your child a dog on the condition that he or she take care of it, how long did the child keep his or her part of the bargain? Is your youngster an artistic child — likes to draw or paint? Unusually creative? Sensitive? Imaginative? Interested in music? Good in math? Is your youngster good in individual sports? Good in dancing? Gymnastics?

If your answer is yes to any one or all of the above, the chances are good that your youngster will do well in learning to ride and probably will always be interested in horses, even if horses do not maintain top priority. If your child is a girl, the odds are even better that she will continue this interest for years, and perhaps become an excellent horsewoman.

Even if your youngster is keen on horses for only a year or so and you have encouraged your child during this time, your time will have been well spent. A parent can do much worse than foster each interest that catches his child's attention — you never know which one will take root and grow. In this age of preoccupation with computers, video tapes, and compact disks, it's good for a young person to have an outdoor activity like riding.

If you go to a local stables to watch a riding class, you will notice that there are about five girl students to every boy student. I have a theory why more girls than boys are involved in riding, and it has nothing to do with any rude Freudian suggestions such as those I have heard in the past. It is related to the rider's sensitivity to the horse.

Most boys have a tendency to ride without caring how the horse feels or what is going on in the horse's head. Those boys are interested primarily in establishing dominance over the horse.

Now it *is* important that the horse understand that he is to obey his rider, that the rider is boss. But there are different kinds of bosses — some you would enjoy working for, and others you would not. The reactions of horses seem to be very much like human reactions. The horse can feel the same way about his rider as a person can about his boss.

When a boy tells the horse, "You do this! Now! Because I said so!", just to show him who's boss, the horse usually resents it. The horse says to himself, "Oh yeah?" and he doesn't perform willingly. If the horse is not well-trained, he might even fight back. The boy will not get much satisfaction from the performance and often figures it's not worth the trouble.

Sometimes the boy has seen enough John Wayne movies so that he thinks of a horse as a four-legged hot-rod. Or he feels the need to build a macho image of himself and he doesn't care how he establishes dominance over the horse. A horse ridden in this manner will never perform as smoothly as it would if approached differently. A ballet dancer who is trained by being whipped will never dance as beautifully as one who performs for the love of it.

Steve, 11, and his Welsh pony, Clay, are proud to carry the American flag in the parade. Not every horse would be that calm and willing.

Girls, on the other hand, usually approach the horse as though he were some great gorgeous creature whom it is their privilege to ride. Girls say, "Oh, you are beautiful! Let's do this....and this....together." The horse responds much as a person would. "Of course! I'd like that!"

When you encounter a boy who *is* tuned in to the horse, who really cares what the horse is thinking, he usually is an extraordinarily good rider. So you won't find as many boys as girls riding in the lessons at the stables, but the boys who are there are usually very very good at it.

From this point on in the book, to avoid having to write "he or she" and "him or her," I shall simplify the use of pronouns by referring to the parent as "he" and to the child or youngster as "she." Because the youngsters who are horse-crazy include ages from the very young up through the teens, I will refer to *all* of them as "kids."

You may already have heard, "The outside of a horse is good for the inside of a man." This is true for children, too, when the horse is really the kid's project and not the parent's. Caring for a horse usually develops a strong sense of responsibility. Horses can and do sometimes present problems. A kid who loves her horse will want to learn how to cope with these situations herself.

Involvement with horses opens the door to a new and exciting world for your kid, a world that can ease the parent's mind. When your kid is on the phone for hours, you'll have a good idea of what she's talking about. If she isn't home very much, you can bet you know where she is. And when she does come home, with muddy boots and horsey-smelling clothes and a shining face, she'll probably be dying to give you a blow by blow description of everything that happened at the stables. Well, almost everything.

A good ride on a good horse can produce a natural high that is extremely exhilarating. When you experience this high, you can dismount and feel that you haven't touched the ground — you're walking three feet above it. Eventually the high wears off, but you still have a tremendous glow of satisfaction. Your self-image is brighter. The kid who once discovers this high can hardly wait to get back on board the horse and find it again. This kind of experience leads to what is called "positive addiction."

Caring for a horse doesn't leave much room for negative addiction. In fourteen years of operating our horsemanship camp, we had only one student who was involved with drugs. She didn't come to camp because she loved horses, but because she wanted to get away from home. It doesn't take a kid long to discover that she can get a horse to do his best only when *she* is at her best — mentally and physically.

What better way to build a healthy and happy life?

At a well-known riding school several years ago I was sitting on a bench watching some thirty horses going around the ring, each with

The family Quarter Horse, Molly, is more fun than a jungle gym for Katy, age four.

a rather small rider on top. The woman next to me was leaning forward anxiously, watching one horse in particular carrying a little bit of a girl. After a while the woman sighed and settled back, smiling, apparently satisfied. She remarked, "Well, I guess Julie's going to be all right."

"Is Julie your little girl?" I asked.

"Oh no," the woman replied quickly. "Julie's our horse. She's brought up three of our children. If she can just bring up one more, that's all I ask."

Chapter 2

From Romance
To Reality

*The gap between the dream and the reality. . . . learn first
and buy later. . . . two types of riding. . . . Western and
English, saddles and sports. . . . safe ways of bridging the
gap: 4-H Clubs; U.S. Pony Clubs. . . . if none are available.*

Even though a kid is completely hooked on horses, reads everything
she can about them, talks horses, and thinks horses, she can be completely unaware of a large gap between her romantic idea of a horse,
and what the horse is really like.

If your kid is an urban child who has had little or no exposure to
horses, the gap may be tremendous. Bridging the gap between romance
and reality can be a positive experience leading to a happy relationship with a horse, or it can be a disaster.

I answered the front doorbell one evening to discover a mother and
daughter standing there. The mother's face was pale and anxious; the
kid's face was pale but determined. The kid had a bandage over her
forehead, a black eye, a bruised cheek, a cut and swollen lip, and one
arm in a sling.

The mother said, "I think she needs riding lessons."

The mother was right.

They had bought their fourteen-year-old daughter a horse several
days before, through an ad in a newspaper. The horse had been trailered
home for the girl the preceding day. This morning the girl had started
off on her horse, bareback, down the driveway. When they reached
the street, the horse whirled and dumped her and ran back to his shed.

Being thrown onto a paved street is no joke; the girl was lucky to be able to get up and walk, and to ride to the hospital in a car instead of an ambulance. X-rays showed no broken bones, but she did have a bad sprain.

I wish this were an unusual situation, but unfortunately it is typical. It's funny how many parents believe in piano lessons, dancing lessons, and driving lessons for their kids, but when it comes to riding a horse, they think their kids are naturals.

You wouldn't turn your kid loose in a swimming pool by herself to learn how to swim—you would find a good swimming teacher. You wouldn't give your kid some skis and put her on a mountain top and expect her to teach herself to ski—you'd see that she had good instruction. Neither should you turn your kid loose on a horse and expect her to teach herself to ride—she needs help in order to ride properly and to avoid accidents.

There are a number of safe and reasonable ways of introducing your kid to the reality of horses, *but starting out by buying a horse for her is not one of them*. I don't need to remind you that one usually learns to drive before one buys a car. It is true that once in a while buying a horse turns out to be the ONLY alternative, and we will deal with that later. A horse is NOT like a bicycle—you can't turn it over to your kid and expect the kid to figure out how to ride it. A horse is more like another kid himself—in fact, more like a thousand-pound kid, a kindergartner, with his own ideas of how to get along in this world. I strongly suggest that your kid ride first and buy later.

Riding for a year or so before the kid gets her own horse has several advantages. It will show you how dedicated the kid is—how much time and effort she will put into riding. This will help you, the parent, to determine how much you want to invest. It also gives the kid a chance to find out what type of riding appeals to her most. Later, if you do decide to buy a horse, you'll know what kind to look for.

Another consideration is that almost any horse that is safe enough for a kid to learn to ride by herself will probably be outgrown in a year or so. The kid will then want a horse that is more of a challenge. Unfortunately, the kid is usually more willing to part with a sister or a brother than with her first horse. You might want to think about that.

Before we discuss some safe and logical ways of introducing the reality of horses to your kid, you should know that there are two general types of riding—English and Western. The activities that the rider wants to take part in will determine whether to ride Western or English. In some sports, like trail riding or endurance riding, the horseman can ride either way. The difference between the two is mainly in the kind of saddle used, the Western saddle or the English saddle. There is also a difference in the bit that the horse carries in his mouth and in the way that the rider handles the reins. The bit is not always indicative, because some

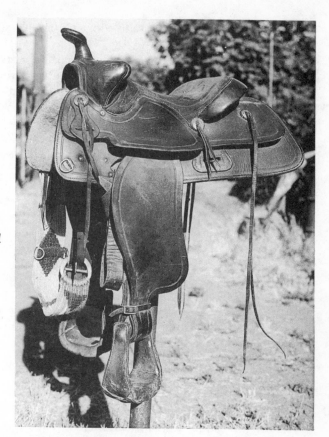

The Western saddle is the one used by all the cowboys in John Wayne movies. Notice the deep seat which gives security to the rider, and the horn and pommel used in roping cattle.

Western riders use a mild English bit.

The easiest way to tell the difference is to look at the saddle. The one you see cowboys using in the "Wild West" movies is the Western or stock saddle. Early Mexican horsemen took the old Spanish saddle and made it bigger and stronger for roping wild cattle. In order to dally the lasso, they devised the horn, a protrusion at the front of the saddle. American cowboys made the saddle lighter but raised and swelled the front part of the saddle supporting the horn to give a more secure seat on a lively horse going after a lively cow. Many people prefer the stock saddle for trail riding because of the security the seat offers. The horn is also useful for a rider to hold on to.

A stock saddle is usually large and heavy, with stirrups of curved wood, sometimes covered with stitched leather, and suspended from wide leather straps called fenders. Western saddles are now built in different styles for specialties in Western riding. They can weigh from 20 pounds for endurance riding and barrel racing to 35 or 40 pounds for roping. A parade saddle loaded with silver for ornamentation can weigh nearly 150 pounds. The stock saddle for ordinary pleasure riding weighs from 32 to 36 pounds.

Several modern sports have evolved from the work of the original cowboy and still use cattle, such as roping, cutting, and team penning. Some of the Western show classes performed without cattle are equitation, trail horse, stock horse, pole bending, and barrel racing.

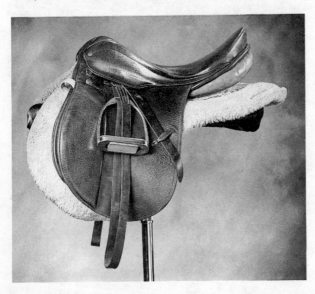

This English saddle is an all-purpose saddle. Because it has longer flaps and knee rolls, it can be used for dressage as well as stadium jumping and cross-country jumping.

The English saddle is smaller and lighter than the Western saddle. The front or pommel rises only a little in front of the rider, and the back or cantle slopes gently up and away from the rider. The stirrups, called irons, are of polished steel or chrome, and hang from narrow leather straps called leathers. The English saddle is usually of softer leather and may have a more padded seat. There are fewer layers of leather between horse and rider, especially in the leg area. Some horsemen who ride both English and Western say they feel "closer" to the horse in an English saddle and can communicate more easily with the horse.

English saddles come in a variety of styles for the many kinds of English sports and equitation. Jumping, hunting, polo, and racing are well known; dressage is a form of artistic riding achieved through systematic training; Eventing or Combined Training is a combination of dressage, cross-country and stadium jumping; saddle seat is riding specially-gaited horses; endurance riding requires miles of hard riding within a specified time limit.

An English saddle for all-purpose riding weighs around 18 pounds. The Western and the English saddle were crossed to produce a

The great variety of horse sports means there is something for every horse-crazy kid to enjoy.

lightweight saddle for endurance riding. An interesting alternative is the Australian saddle. Developed by the cowboys for use in the rugged outback while herding sheep and cattle, it drew attention in the film, "The Man From Snowy River." Because of its comfort and practicality, it has grown in popularity ever since, particularly for endurance riding.

As you visit stables and riding schools with your kid, you will soon be able to pick out which riders are riding English and which are riding Western. You will see which saddles are preferred for the different sports. Of course if a rider is bareback you'll have to watch how the person rides to know whether his style is Western or English. That takes practice.

If a kid has not had any previous contact with horses, it is possible that she will be overwhelmed by the actual size and strength of a horse. A good approach is to visit some projects where children are involved having fun with horses while they are learning. Two nationally known organizations offering such projects are the 4-H Clubs and the U.S. Pony Clubs, Inc. If the reality turns out to be more than your kid can handle, she won't tell you, but you'll know. She'll stop needling you to buy a horse, and there will be some conversations in which horses are not mentioned once, and her face won't light up like a light bulb when a horse is flashed on the TV screen. But don't count on it.

The 4-H movement was begun by the Department of Agriculture in 1907 to offer youngsters in rural communities a type of education more directly useful than that offered by the public schools. 4-H Clubs are sponsored by the State and can be located through the County Farm Advisor's Office of the Agricultural Department. You can also find 4-H listed in the white pages of your telephone book if there is a club in your county. Some communities have a large number of 4-H Clubs, and each club will have a number of projects with project leaders. There will be a beef leader, a sheep leader, etc., and hopefully a horse leader, depending on the area in which you are located. In 4-H, children may ride either Western or English. The program is open to all children entering 4th grade and above, or from 9 to 18 years of age.

The 4-H program has two brief manuals on horses at an adult reading level. No textbook written for children is available at this time. The horse leaders usually are horse trainers involved in horse showing. Recently more emphasis is being placed upon care of the horse and horsemanship.

As horse projects increase in numbers, more parents are becoming involved as leaders. Meetings are monthly, and offer unmounted lessons in the proper care of a horse, and mounted lessons for riding. Some leaders encourage children without horses to attend the meetings so that when they do get a horse they will know how to take care of it.

Six levels of horsemanship are outlined, and a child can progress informally from one to another at his own speed and ability. To acquire some of the material if there is no 4-H Club in your area, contact the U.S. Department of Agriculture in your state, or your State Land-Grant University, or write directly to the National 4-H Council, 7100 Connecticut Avenue, Chevy Chase, Maryland 20815.

The United States Pony Clubs, Inc., is a non-profit educational organization begun in 1929 by the British Horse Society. In England, all classes for riders under 21 years of age are called Pony Classes, regardless of the size of their mounts. The Pony Club was founded to teach children how to care properly for horses when they could not afford to keep them at a stables, but could have them in their back yards. The organization has been so successful that at present 30 countries in the free world participate in the Pony Club program.

The United States joined the program in 1953, incorporated in Massachusetts, and member clubs now number more than 400 across the country. They teach riding, mounted sports, and the care of horses and ponies to all children under the age of 21.

Pony Club teaches only English riding. The program has nine levels of ability called ratings, with well-defined standards for each level. Members progress from one rating to another by taking the examination for the next level when they feel they are ready. Each examination includes written work, stable management, and three riding tests. All members begin as "unrated." Examinations for the first five levels are given by local Pony Club Examiners; the sixth is given by a Regional Examiner. The three highest levels, which represent a very high degree of proficiency, are judged by two or more National Examiners. Only a few Pony Clubbers are able to achieve those levels. Most who do are Olympic material. Many of our U.S. Equestrian Team members got their start in the U.S. Pony Clubs.

The offical textbook is the *Manual of Horsemanship* of the Pony Club. It is an excellent reference book for any horse person, child or adult. If you cannot locate it at your local bookstore or tack store, you can send to the National Office for it. To locate the Pony Club nearest you and to get the textbook, write to the United States Pony Clubs, Inc., whose current address and phone number are in the Resource Guide. They also have pamphlets telling about the Pony Club, how to start one, a list of publications available, and other information which they will be happy to send you at nominal cost.

With some kids, the prior amount of exposure to horses doesn't matter at all. We had an eleven-year-old enroll at camp whose entire experience consisted of a few pony rides in the park—the kind where the pony goes around on a small circular track.

This kid was about four-and-a-half feet high and weighed less than sixty pounds, but she took to horses like peanut butter takes to jelly. Her school horse was in heaven. He'd never had so much attention. When she wasn't riding him, he was being brushed and combed and washed and polished and given so many goodies that he fairly glowed with happiness. His paddock was the cleanest, his water tub the brightest, his tack the shiniest, of all the horses. When the kid couldn't find anything else to do for her horse, she'd sit on the top rail and sing to him. He loved it. We had to pry her out of his paddock at night to send her to bed. This kid has now gone through college and is a lovely young lady and she still loves horses.

Be forewarned—your kid may not know any more than that kid to start with, but she may become just as devoted.

If neither 4-H nor Pony Club is in your locality, it will be up to you, the conscientious parent, to do some homework for the sake of your horse-crazy kid. Your homework will consist of exploring different stables and barns, investigating summer camps and riding schools, and watching a lot of instructors in action as they teach and ride. It's not just for your kid's pleasure, *it's for her safety.*

Deciding whether to ride Western or English is not nearly as important as finding a GOOD teacher. The sad fact is that ANYONE WHO WANTS TO TEACH RIDING CAN DO SO, REGARDLESS OF HIS EXPERIENCE OR ABILITY. That is why it is so difficult to find a *good* teacher.

If you don't know how to ride and have had little or no experience with horses, how do you know what constitutes a good teacher? How do you find one?

I will give you some guidelines in the next chapter.

Chapter 3

Doing Your Homework

No teaching requirements . . . . the ideal teacher . . . . 5 kinds of stables: riding clubs, riding schools and academies, training stables, boarding stables, rental stables.

Most horse-crazy kids are so eager to get to a horse that the qualifications of the teacher seem irrelevant to them. "My friend Margie's got a horse, and she'll teach me to ride," is a typical suggestion. It may sound like a good idea, but it's not. Would you want your ten-year-old taking swimming lessons from a ten-year-old who is just learning to swim? Both situations can lead to disaster.

You may not have a great deal of choice in instructors or places where your kid can ride. It's possible to draw a blank. Or maybe you live in the country, and when you ask about riding lessons everybody doubles up with laughter. We'll deal with that later. Let's look first at the ideal situation, and then we'll have a better idea of how to cope with reality.

A good riding instructor is very much like any good teacher—he knows his subject matter well, he cares a great deal about his students, and he enjoys teaching.

For a riding instructor to know his subject matter well, he must have had years of riding and working with *many different horses and people* in his riding discipline. This is essential to keeping physical risk for the student to a minimum. Riding just one horse over the years won't do.

An instructor who cares for his students will want success for each student in relation to the student's desire and ability. Some children are very competitive, and they will thrive on the challenge of competi-

The right kind of instruction can turn beginning riders into good ones, and even eliminate bad riding habits.

tion in gymkhanas or horse showing or endurance riding. Others will be happy if they can just go trail riding with a friend or two. A good instructor won't push all his students into the show ring, but help each one on the road the student chooses.

Last of all, a teacher who enjoys his work can better motivate students to do their best. It's easier to pull a chain than to push it, and a teacher who inspires his students to follow him is far better than the one who drives his students. As you can imagine, the ideal instructor is hard to find, but there are many teachers with whom your child will be safe and can learn the basics of good horsemanship. If you find an instructor for your kid with the three ideal qualities, you are ahead of the game.

Where do you look for a teacher like this?

To start teaching in our public schools, a person must earn a Teacher's Certificate in the State where he wishes to teach, showing he has fulfilled certain requirements in education and experience.

There is nothing like that for teaching riding. In fact, not one of the fifty States has established *any* requirements for riding instructors. In England, it's not the government but the British Horse Society which has a system for certifying different levels of riding instructors as they emerge from certain schools. Unfortunately, the United States has no such system.

Many riding schools in the U.S. offer certificates of ability. There are as many different certificates as there are schools, and fulfilling the requirements varies from a few days to several years.

The oldest national organization with uniform standards for certification in horsemanship is the United States Pony Club. Their rating system is an accurate indication of the level of achievement. Any Pony Clubber, for example, who has achieved an HA rating has had to demonstrate a high proficiency in both riding and teaching for many years.

In 1967, a non-profit organization called the Camp Horsemanship Association was founded to establish national standards for instruction and promote safer camp programs in horsemanship. The organization holds Riding Instructor Clinics throughout the United States and Canada as well as a yearly National Instructor Certification Clinic.

The organization has contributed greatly to improving technical skills as well as safety standards in many stables and camps through their educational program. Their series of excellent instruction manuals are highly readable even for young children and are available to the public. For more information, write to the Camp Horsemanship Association, listed in the Resource Guide.

In spite of the educational programs in existence, the unfortunate truth is that at present anyone who wants to teach riding can do so, regardless of experience or ability. Many instructors learned to ride by the seat of their pants and what their next-door neighbor told them, and that neighbor learned the same way from *his* neighbor, and so on. And if the first neighbor didn't know much to begin with. . . .

Let's assume that you do have some choices, and that you're willing to check out the possibilities as you would in any school situation. Of course one of the first places to look is at a stables. That's when you discover that just as there are different kinds of schools, like prep schools, business schools, beauty schools, and medical assistant schools, there are different kinds of stables.

Stables fall into one of five types and combinations of these types: *riding clubs, riding schools or academies, training stables, boarding stables,* and *rental stables.* There also are breeding farms or stables, but we will not discuss them here because they seldom offer riding lessons.

A *riding club* is like a country club for riders instead of golfers or tennis players. There is usually an initiation fee, monthly membership dues, a resident "pro" (the riding master or resident trainer), a teaching staff, stables where members can keep their horses, and the opportunity to use its beautifully maintained facilities.

The latter can include riding rings, dressage arenas, gymkhana arenas (for pole bending, barrel racing, etc.), jumping arenas, turn-out paddocks, hot walkers, and even polo fields. A turn-out paddock is a fenced area where a horse confined to a stall most of the time can be turned out to romp and play and exercise. A hot walker is a machine faintly resembling a merry-go-round to which four horses at a time can be attached and be made to walk leisurely in a circle. A hot walker is used primarily for cooling out a horse hot from exercise, and occasionally for giving a horse some exercise without riding him. Some riding clubs which specialize in Western riding have cattle for the members to use in practicing roping, cutting, or penning of calves.

Only members can board their horses at the private club. Boarding means providing the horse's basic feed and a place for him to live. For an additional fee, members can have their horses groomed, tacked up (prepared for riding), even exercised or ridden, and put away. This service is a great convenience for the busy people who feel that a little time in the saddle is better than none, and can afford this service. A few clubs permit non-members to bring their horses to the club for instruction from their staff.

Most clubs expect their members to own or lease the horses that they ride, but might have a few school horses for members to use while they are looking for a horse.

Riding clubs are usually very beautiful places, expensive to belong to, open only by invitation, and furnish excellent instruction, especially for those who wish to be involved in horse showing. More about that later.

Riding schools and *academies* are primarily teaching institutions with horses. Their purpose is to teach the non-rider to ride, and to improve the skills of advanced riders. Such stables usually have many good school horses and a teaching staff experienced in handling the different levels of horsemanship. Students and sometimes non-students can board horses at the school.

Colleges and universities with a horse science program often also operate a riding school. Many of the riding classes may be open to persons not enrolled in the college.

A few riding schools *require* a student to take a certain number of lessons each month to maintain higher standards of horsemanship.

Training stables are operated by persons who train horses and who teach the riders whose horses are being trained. A horse doesn't change from a frolicking green colt into a dependable riding horse by accident. The horse needs lessons too—from an expert. A poorly-trained horse is much harder to handle than a poorly-trained kid. Young horses can think up as many things to do as kids can in school, and horses are bigger and stronger.

There's no membership required for keeping your horse at a training stables—only payment of the boarding and training fees. A trainer "schools" a horse to increase his value, or to make him ridable for an owner who has neither the time nor the skill for training the horse himself. Usually this kind of stables boards only those horses which are in training. Most of these horses are being prepared for entering horse shows, either in "halter classes" where the horse is judged while being led, or in "performance classes" where the horse is judged while being ridden.

Horse shows are commonly used as a yardstick for measuring the trainer's ability as well as the ability of the horse or rider. At stables keyed to horse showing, the trainer is often like a football coach. A highly competitive trainer will map out a campaign of shows suitable for his students, accompany the students and their horses to the shows, and coach them to get through the game. The more ribbons brought home by riders at a particular stable, the greater the reputation of that trainer.

Boarding stables are operated for the boarding of horses whose owners cannot or do not wish to keep them on their own property. Again, there is no membership involved, only the payment of the board bill, usually a month in advance. In many areas, good boarding stables are scarce, and often have a waiting list for their stalls or paddocks. Increasing population and rising real estate values continue to convert stable land into housing developments.

Most boarding stables have a number of instructors on the premises. How well qualified they are is another matter. At some stables, anyone who boards a horse there is allowed to teach as long as the lessons don't interfere with other riders. Frequently riders who have had three or four lessons on a horse will feel competent enough to teach their friends how to ride. That's not what you are looking for.

Other stables control the teaching, knowing that a good instructor is a drawing card for boarders, and poor instructors are a hazard. Some stables have a financial arrangement with the instructor, varying from the teacher's giving the manager a percentage of his teaching income to guaranteeing that a certain number of stalls will always be occupied by horses of the trainer's students. A well-run boarding stables will have several good instructors on the premises, and will not let others teach there.

Rental stables are those where all the horses are the property of the stable manager or owner. He rents out the horses by the hour, half-day, or day, to anyone who is willing to pay. Some stables require an attendant to accompany the riders ("guided rides only") with a minimum number in each group that goes out on the trail. There are a few stables which permit the persons renting the horses to ride out without a guide, as long as they are back at a certain time. The horses at rental stables are almost always tacked up with Western bridles and saddles.

Resort areas and vacation spots frequently have rental stables for vacationers who enjoy trail riding. Resort area horses are usually well-mannered, well-cared-for, and trained to walk head-to-tail with the horse in front. Very few of these stables permit their horses to go out without a guide, as much for the protection of the horse as for the rider. Such places may advertise trail rides, cook-outs, barbecues, and other diversions, including moonlight rides when the moon is full. This is fine recreation, but the guide or wrangler seldom has time for giving riding instruction except those basics necessary for the safe return of both horse and rider.

The horses at rental stables in or near towns and cities are very different from those at resort stables. City riders aren't looking for a leisurely trail ride to enjoy the scenery. Usually their idea of a ride is to get on a horse and hopefully look like John Wayne. They want to gallop off in all directions. Most riders of rental horses know little or nothing about riding, and without meaning to, often abuse the horses.

Rental horses have to be tough, physically and mentally, to protect themselves from well-intentioned but ignorant riders. These horses develop incredibly strong neck muscles and high head carriages and the ability to ball up their tongues in order to protect their mouths from the harsh and frequent jerks on the reins. They also develop sides of iron so the constant kicks won't bother them. Last of all, they have clocks built inside their heads so they know when half the time is up for which they have been rented. Then they will turn around and head for the barn.

Because of the temperament and experience of rental horses, very few are suitable as school horses, and lessons are seldom available at rental stables. It is difficult to do much with a horse who has learned through bitter experience to ignore his rider if he wants to survive.

There are exceptions to every rule. Occasionally you will find a rental stable with a horse or two not yet disillusioned by the human race, and those horses can be used as school horses. Instruction at those stables might consist of telling the rider to sit up straight, kick the horse to start, and point with the reins in the direction the rider wants to go. This isn't teaching horsemanship.

Stables can also be combinations of these five types. Boarding and training are frequently combined in a stable. The yellow pages of almost every telephone book in the United States has two listings which can help you find instruction. They are "Riding Academies" and—surprise: "Stables." The phone book is just for starters. Sometimes good stables and excellent instructors aren't even listed in the yellow pages. I'll show you how to track those down.

I suggest you go through the yellow pages and make a list of the names and phone numbers of all the stables which look promising for teaching your kid. You could omit rental stables, stables which have training only, and perhaps private riding clubs, depending upon your budget. Even if you have an expandable wallet, it's a good idea to keep costs down until your kid proves that she is dedicated.

The yellow pages also list tack stores and feed stores. These often have bulletin boards with business cards of local instructors. Add the business cards to your collection. There are also a number of very fine riders who run training and teaching operations at their own barns. They don't advertise much because they usually have all the students or horses they can handle. Their reputations get around by word of mouth, but they might post a business card at the local feed stores. When you go to visit them you should be able to separate the strictly amateur teachers from the good instructors, by what they say as well as the way they teach. Even the Chamber of Commerce can be helpful if they have a list of horse organizations in the community. Members of horse clubs are known for their eagerness to enlist others in their sport, and you may get more suggestions than you care to follow.

Sooner or later you will meet a persuasive horseman who tells you that buying a horse for your kid to learn on is by far the best way to go—and he just happens to have for sale the perfect horse for your kid. A firm "no thank you" may well save you hours of anguish, not to mention money.

Now telephone each stable or barn on your list and ask to talk to the manager or instructor. KEEP A WRITTEN RECORD OF THE

RESULTS. After you have called three or four stables they all begin to sound alike. Pretty soon you wonder if it was the Foggy Bottom Barn that had the Pony Club instructor, and the Giddy-Yup Stables that had the ex-barrel racing champion teacher, or was it the other way around?

Ask if lessons are offered, what kind (Western or English), the *type* of instruction (equitation, saddle seat, dressage, jumping, etc.) and if private or class instruction is available. Ask about the rates, and if there is more than one instructor at that barn. Last of all, ask when the classes are held so you can visit them. You can eliminate some stables by one phone call.

Suppose you've read this whole chapter and you realize in despair that there are practically no stables to choose from. But you do want your kid to learn how to ride. Weekly lessons are a gradual and sound way for a kid to learn, but they're not the only way.

One of the best alternatives to weekly riding lessons is the summer camp. In fact, if your child has had no real exposure to horses, this can be an excellent way to close the gap between romance and reality. Riding every day instead of once a week is a demanding exercise when your kid isn't used to it, but the effort pays off. We'll explore summer camps, too.

Whether you have a nice list of promising stables to visit right now, or have opted for a camp next summer, it's important to know what to look for when you make your first "field trip" with your kid to a place that gives lessons. The next chapter will give you some interesting pointers.

Chapter 4

Ten Easy Lessons Or Five Hard Ones

What to look for at stables....weekly lessons.... summer programs....day camps....resident camps.... accredited school programs.

Kids love field trips. Your kid will especially love a field trip for visiting a riding class, but you'll have work to do. You need to be as picky in choosing a stables for riding lessons as you would in selecting a swimming school. *Safety for your kid comes first.*

Dress comfortably and wear sensible shoes—no open toes. Be sure that your kid is wearing sensible shoes too. Sandals and bare feet are a no-no around horses.

Your general impression of the stables is important. Ask yourself if this is the kind of place where you'd like your kid to spend a lot of time, because she will. Do the stables look well-cared-for and properly maintained? Are there other children around? Do those children not in the lessons or taking care of horses have adult supervision?

Walk around the stables without trying to make friends with any of the horses. Be sure your own kid stays with you and doesn't dash off to pat horses. Strange horses can have bad habits, such as nipping.

Are the barns and fences in good repair? The stables and paddocks should be clean with wide aisles wherever horses have to be led. No wheelbarrows should be left in the aisle, no tools and equipment that could hurt a horse if one gets loose and runs around. The various arenas for riding should be well-fenced, and posted with ring rules. ("No running of horses; no sitting on the rail," etc.)

Take a good look at the horses. They should be healthy-looking—eyes bright, ears alert, no runny noses, no ribs showing, the feet trimmed and neat-looking without chips and cracks. Any cuts or skinned places on the horses should have been treated recently.

When a lesson begins, stay away from the rail and find a place to sit and watch. Do the kids look like they are having a good time? Are most of them relaxed and happy, or tense and scared? Do the kids get to ride or are they mostly lectured while they sit on the horses?

Does the instructor shout and yell a lot? Or is his manner one that gives confidence and inspiration to the kids? Does he let a kid know when she's doing well?

Does the instructor give equal time to each student? One or two will always need extra help, but you don't want to see favoritism, especially when the determining factor might be the amount of money the kid's family can spend.

If there are other parents around, ask them how they feel about the instructor. Are their kids enthusiastic or do they feel frustrated? Do the parents think that their kids are making steady progress?

If the class is in English riding and any jumping is involved, is every student wearing a safety helmet with a full harness under the chin, not just an elastic band? If the answer is no—*scratch that instructor from your list.* The current rules of the U.S. Pony Club, Inc., for a very sound reason, require that all riders wear an approved helmet with full harness in place *at all times when mounted,* whether or not they are jumping. That rule has prevented many serious injuries. It is a rule that all knowledgeable instructors will observe in their daily lessons *certainly when any jumping is involved,* and *preferably all the time when mounted.* There are even clear plastic harnesses to meet the "vanity" requirements of the younger set.

When the class is over, watch how the kids handle their mounts. Are the horses turned over to grooms, or are the kids allowed to groom their horses? Your kid will learn a lot more about riding if she is taught to take care of her horse, but not all instructors have time.

A well-established stable or riding school generally is particular about its teaching staff. If a stables has an instructor with a good national reputation, you'll probably hear good things about him long before you get there.

But for those instructors about whom little is said or known, find a time when the instructor can talk with you. Ask him to tell you about himself: how he started riding, what different kinds of horses he has ridden, how long he has been teaching, what his specialty is, what he would like to do. A good instructor should not mind this inquiry—

after all, your kid's welfare will be in his hands.

For beginning students, an instructor does not have to be an outstanding rider, but he must have achieved a certain degree of facility on a number of different horses. There is absolutely no substitute for experience, like hours behind a wheel to become a good driver. The longer a person has been riding and teaching, the better his chances of coping with any unusual situation that arises. No matter how well-trained a horse is, sooner or later he will behave like a horse. Your kid needs a teacher who can deal wisely with the unexpected.

A top-ranked rider is not necessarily a good teacher, especially for beginners. Sometimes a gifted rider has difficulty teaching kids who learn at a normal rate. If a kid should demonstrate a lot of talent, it's important to find a teacher who can make the most of her ability without pushing her too fast. A solid foundation in the basics is essential for excellence in higher levels.

A good teacher can put himself in the kid's place and know when it is good to move the kid ahead to something new, when to back off and let her become more sure of herself, and when to inspire her to be bold. A good teacher takes his time and doesn't rush his students into new things like quicker spins or higher fences for fear that if he doesn't, the kid will lose interest and go somewhere else. The teacher who asks a student to jump fences for which she is not really ready is a threat to the rider and to the sport, but I have seen it done, a lot.

Some teachers will rattle off all the "greats" they have trained with. "Trained with" may mean they have ridden past the arena where that person was teaching. There are teachers who spend most of the class time talking on the telephone while one of the students in the class "teaches" the class for him. Lesson time should be sacred to the teacher and the students. If you phone the instructor at the stables and the response is, "He's teaching. Can he call you back?" that's an encouraging sign.

I once asked a youngster who was teaching riding to her friends if she were still taking riding lessons. She said, "Oh no, I learned to ride last year." She didn't realize that it's what you learn after you know it all that counts.

Riding is like many other skills—the more you learn, the more there is to learn. Reiner Klimke, who has been one of the world's greatest dressage riders for many years, was asked after he won the Gold Medal at the Los Angeles Olympics, how long it took him to learn to ride. He replied, "I'm still learning."

If you are fortunate enough to have different stables to visit and instructors to watch, you may find that your kid is drawn to one particular teacher even though that type of riding isn't what either of you originally had in mind. That's a good place to start. What appeals to her may not appeal to you, but she is the one who will be in the saddle.

Choosing to go Western or go English is not an irrevocable decision. A rider can change from one to the other, and many riders enjoy both. It is fairly easy to switch from Western riding to English riding. It is even easier to switch from English to Western. Some English schools use a Western saddle for a total beginner because there's more to hang on to; after the kid has learned the basics she is put in an English saddle. Other schools use the English saddle from the beginning. Riding is a balance sport, like ballet, gymnastics, bicycling, skiing, and skating. If your kid is already proficient in one of these sports, she will probably learn to ride more quickly than someone who has not had that exposure.

One more element is absolutely vital to your kid's safety. Even if the instructor is excellent, the horse that your kid rides in the lesson can be the deciding factor in how much progress she can make.

When it comes to the nitty gritty of learning to ride, there are only two kinds of horses—those that are *safe* to learn to ride on, and those that are *not*. The unsafe ones are frequently found listed for sale in the classified ads. The safe ones, regardless of appearance, are not only hard to find but are worth their weight in gold.

In a later chapter we will discuss different kinds of horses, and in particular those that are safe to learn to ride on. For now, we shall assume that the good instructor also has available a good horse that lets your kid think about herself and her riding position without having to worry about keeping the horse under control.

If you find an instructor whom you like, go ahead and sign up your kid for her first lesson—one week at a time. Most schools require that the kid take at least one private lesson before the kid enters a class. This one-on-one arrangement helps the teacher see what kind of student he will be working with (such as timid or bold) so he can better match the school horse to the rider. Any time you stay to watch a lesson, *don't say a word* to your kid or to the teacher until the lesson is over.

There may be a big difference between the horse in your kid's mind, and the REAL THING. A child can be truly overwhelmed by the reality, so listen to her carefully after the first lesson. Listen to what she doesn't say as well as what she does. If she loved it, you'll know.

If riding lessons in your area are not feasible, or if your child is still interested in horses but perhaps a little reluctant after her first lesson, a summer camp may be a good choice. Not a horsemanship camp, but one that offers other activities as well as horseback riding. There can be crafts, swimming, hiking, team sports, etc. Both day camps and resident camps have good programs.

At a camp with a well-rounded program, the daily riding instruction is usually an informal affair, with children in various stages of excitement, counselors with patience and lots of enthusiasm, and a "string" of school horses most of whom truly love to haul little kids around and be adored by them. The horses are chosen not because of their looks but because they are safe for beginners, and they come with names like Socks, Bucky (a buckskin color, not one that bucks), Red, Cherokee, Prince, Susie, and Snowball.

These kids will never forget the thrill of riding bareback across the hills at their camp.

Instead of saddles the horses may wear bareback pads, safer and much easier for children to handle, and English bridles with snaffle bits or Western bridles with mild curb bits. The children are taught how to brush a horse and get him ready for riding, and are given the basics of riding so they can go on trail rides and feel good about it. The more experienced kids may get to play games on horseback.

There's one thing that doesn't happen often, but it can—a kid will discover that taking care of a real horse and learning to ride it are not nearly as much fun as she had thought it would be. She wrinkles up her nose at picking up ma-noo-noo (sometimes called manure) on a rake. Brushing a horse, even with the wind blowing the right way, becomes a terrible chore. As for getting up on top of this enormous animal and trying to tell it what to do, forget it!

The kid can drop out of the riding lessons and still enjoy the rest of the camp program. If this happens to your kid, don't fret about having sent her to camp for nothing. You will have saved yourself a lot of time, effort, and even more money by finding out, early in the game, that you can cross off equine activities from your kid's wish list.

Where do you find the names of good camps?

The best source for camps with varied activities is the American Camping Association, a non-profit professional organization dedicated to organized camping for children and adults. Both day camps and resident camps are listed.

The American Camping Association was founded in 1910 for the purpose of developing standards for camping, and for protecting campers by examining the operation of each camp for acceptable performance. In order to be accredited by the American Camping Association, a camp must fulfil high standards in administration, personnel, and the programs offered. A camp director must meet A.C.A. standards to earn the title of Certified Camp Director (C.C.D.).

The A.C.A. publishes a very complete "Parents' Guide to Accredited Camps" for less than $10.00. You will find their toll free phone number and address at the back of this book under Resource Guide.

There are other camping organizations, such as the Camp Horsemanship Association which lists camps, stables, and schools offering riding programs, and the Association of Independent Camps. To contact these, see the Resource Guide.

Camps located in your area will be listed in the yellow pages under CAMPS. A call to the Girl Scouts, Boy Scouts, YWCA and YMCA might be helpful. If you want to be very thorough, write to the Department of Public Health of the county and ask for a list of all the camps to which they have given licenses. Some counties distribute such a list without charge, and others with large populations charge a fee. The list says nothing about camp programs or the campers accepted, but it will be the most comprehensive list you could possibly acquire. During the long winter evenings you can check them out on the telephone.

The basic philosophy of a private camp and the program offered depend almost entirely on the director and vary tremendously, so it is important to contact each camp which sounds promising. Write for the brochures, and visit the camp if possible before making any decisions.

As for the kid who has already had exposure to real live horses and it only made her more enthusiastic, she may be happy at a camp devoted entirely to a horsemanship program. The kind you are looking for will probably *not* be listed in the ACA booklet. Very few horsemanship camps apply to be accredited by the American Camping Association because their goals are different. Accredited camps focus on social

A horsemanship camp offers intensive learning, with some exposure to the higher levels of riding.

development of the child; horsemanship camps focus on producing good horsemen.

Usually horsemanship camps are operated in conjunction with year-round riding schools. These schools are geared for teaching all levels of horsemanship, from total beginners to advanced riders. They include a complete program of horse care that will prove invaluable if your kid gets more involved with horses.

To find horsemanship camps, contact the same places where you were looking for lessons. The Membership Directory of the Camp Horsemanship Association lists camps that specialize in riding. Most year-round stables offer during the summer a "day-camp" program of daily riding classes, even including horse care and related subjects. Most horse magazines carry ads for horsemanship camps. Check out the land-grant colleges and schools for summer camp programs.

Some of these riding programs are highly specialized and demanding. However, a kid can learn more in two weeks of intensive instruction than she would in many months of once-a-week lessons. You should find out as much as you can about their purpose and program before you enroll your kid.

Now that you are on the verge of having your kid actually getting on board a horse, please don't rush out and buy her some elegant riding clothes. A child beginning ballet lessons doesn't start out with the costume for Swan Lake. Let's look at appropriate clothing in the next chapter.

Chapter 5

Be Smart And Dress The Part

Comfort for riding—safety is vital. . . . footware, English and Western. . . . headgear, English and Western. . . . out-grown riding wear. . . . other clothing. . . . shopping around. . . . catalogues.

James M. Barrie, the creator of the immortal Peter Pan, was also a realist. In an early novel, one of his characters declared in often-quoted words, "You cannot expect to be both grand and comfortable."

There is no question in the mind of the experienced rider—comfort comes first. Few things are more difficult for a rider than trying to tell her horse what to do when she is suffering from blisters on her heels, bruises on her calves, or a cold wind that goes right through her riding shirt. Fortunately, manufacturers of riding apparel are now producing clothing as comfortable as it is attractive and fashionable, and there is a wide choice. A rider *can* be both grand and comfortable, but if there has to be a choice, let it be for comfort.

Most riders have two kinds of clothing—everyday wear for schooling their horses, and more formal wear if they are involved in horse showing of any kind. By the time your kid is ready to compete in horse shows, she will be fairly knowledgeable about dressing for them and will have acquired some of what she needs. In the meantime, clothes for daily riding and schooling need to be comfortable and sturdy.

Both you and your kid will be more comfortable knowing she is dressed for safety as well as for comfort. The first line of safety and comfort is in footware. Your kid needs boots or shoes with hard soles, firm leather across the toes, protection over the instep, and sufficient heel to prevent the foot from sliding all the way into the stirrup. Falling off a horse when a boot is stuck "home" in the stirrup can lead to bloodshed. This means no sandals, tennies, or the popular running and walking shoes unless your kid is riding bareback. Even then there is the danger of being stepped on while working around the horse.

In Western riding, the high heel of the cowboy boot had its origin in safety, and later grew for vanity (too high for comfort in walking). The higher top of the cowboy boot affords protection for the lower leg from friction with the saddle as well as against dense underbrush in rugged country. Western boots come in a wide price range and all sizes, even little bitty boots.

Less expensive than cowboy boots, the Western work boot called "Wellingtons," which apparently originated in England, is a sturdy, comfortable boot with adequate protection in all the proper places and a good heel.

An ankle-length laced Western boot called "packers" are available in different heel and uppers heights. They are practical for both riding and walking.

The high boots for English riding are expensive and in most cases are not practical for growing children. In the East especially, many well-known English trainers encourage their young students to wear short paddock boots instead of high boots, and jodhpurs (pronounced jod-purrs because the "h" comes *before* the "p") instead of breeches. Jodhpurs are a long, comfortably-fitted pant with reinforced calves and knees, a cuff around the lower edge, and an elastic to slip under the boot to keep the pants from riding up the leg. Paddock boots extend just above the ankle and have either laces or elastic inserts at the sides so the boot can easily be slipped on and off. Children smartly turned out in paddock boots and jodhpurs appear at some of the most elegant horse shows.

English high boots are also available in rubber, lined and unlined, some so cleverly made that they look and feel very much like leather. In muddy stable areas these waterproof boots are quite appropriate. They are also inexpensive and can be worn in place of leather riding boots for the budget-conscious rider.

An inexpensive but practical alternative for jodhpurs or breeches in everyday riding are leather leggings, called "short chaps" and "pistols" out West. Pistols cover the leg from ankle to knee, fasten with velcro, and are reinforced on the calf and knee where it is most needed. Worn over ordinary jeans, these are very popular with exercise lads at the race tracks for morning work-outs. Combined with paddock boots or Western boots, leggings offer excellent protection and are more comfortable in hot weather than high leather boots. Long chaps, also called "shotguns," are worn in the show ring for Western classes.

Along with proper footwear, protective headgear should be high in your priorities. Horseback riding is acknowledged to be a high-risk sport, and kids sometimes fall off. The riding helmet with chin harness, approved by the American Horse Shows Association and the U.S. Pony Clubs, Inc., is constructed to stay on the rider's head even if the rider is upside down on her way to the ground. The helmet is designed to help prevent concussions and other head injuries. Cloth covers for the helmets come in many colors and designs, looking much like jockey's caps, and even in black for formal horse shows. Helmets with hard visors are no longer approved although many are still around. Be sure that your kid's helmet has no hard visor, and that the cloth cover has a soft visor that will offer no resistance on contact.

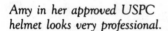
Amy in her approved USPC helmet looks very professional.

English riders have worn safety helmets for years, and now at last a good-looking safety helmet for Western riders has been produced. Looking just like a Western hat, they come in straw or felt, have a fiberglass shell inside, and an adjustable chin strap. Approved by the U.S. Pony Club, they are available in leading tack stores and through some of the principal catalogues. Decreasing the risk of serious injury to their kids should appeal to all parents.

One more safety item is becoming popular especially among riders involved in jumping. It is a back board or body protector, worn under the hunt shirt or jacket, and is an item that lives up to its name. Clearly equestrians are becoming *more* safety conscious, not less. I foresee that some day the safety helmet with chin harness will be required for all riders, Western and English.

Western riders will find jeans are appropriate for almost all their riding. English riders are much more informal than twenty years ago, and usually "dress" only when they are riding in regular classes.

Most children's riding clothes are out-grown before they are worn out. If your kid is going to be with a Pony Club, ask some of the other parents about their kids' out-grown riding clothes. They will probably be delighted to know of a younger kid who can use them. Often a junior riding club in the neighborhood has members whose closets are full of equestrian clothing too small for them. Benefit horse shows frequently have a booth for exchanging riding clothes. Some stables regularly stage "swap meets" for equestrian wear.

If none of these suggestions work out and your kid is growing so fast that you cringe when you look at prices of coats and breeches or jodhpurs, don't give up. Try one of the pattern catalogues and have someone handy with a sewing machine (you?) make your kid a stylish wardrobe at a fraction of the cost.

Riding gloves are helpful not only when it's cold, but when your kid's hands are tender and the reins are dry and stiff from not having been cleaned and oiled as often as they should be. The main requirement for riding gloves is that the fabric, of leather, nylon, or string knit, be thin enough that the rider doesn't lose sensitivity for communicating with the horse through the reins. If your kid is planning to go in for horse showing, wearing gloves during everyday riding will help her to be more comfortable later when she goes in the ring and gloves are required.

The market today offers every kind of clothing imaginable for the aspiring as well as the experienced rider. Undergarmets, regular clothing, and outerwear are available in many materials and styles. Breeches are now made even in denim and in sweats for schooling. There is no reason for your kid to be uncomfortable while she is riding unless she completely misjudges the weather when she starts out. She can always fasten extra clothing to the saddle or around her waist.

It pays to shop around because tack stores vary greatly in their price ranges. Price isn't the only thing to consider. Those with good service rate high on my list because it's not practical to try out some things just in the store. Your kid can't be sure how some items, like bits and saddles and saddle pads, will work out or fit until she's tried them on the horse or ridden with them. I like a tack shop where the owners are happy to exchange or take back an unsuitable item, particularly when it comes to buying tack for the horse.

If you are out in the country or in a town with stores offering little to choose from, turn to the catalogue ads in the national horse magazines. Once you're on the equine catalogue mailing list, you'll be dazzled by the array of items offered. Some catalogues specialize in Western wear, some in English, and others offer both.

Whichever road your kid decides to take in her pursuit of horsemanship, there is also a road for you to travel. Your road leads to being able to help her when she needs it, and to know when to step aside and let her find her own way. The first milestone on your road is learning a little more about this animal that your kid finds so appealing. You'll get an introduction in the next chapter.

Chapter 6

Don't Knock It— He Survived!

Why the horse is spooky. . . .survival by flight. . . .his alarm system. . . .vision. . . .digestive system. . . .the stay apparatus. . . .his hearing. . . .backtracking. . . . how to cope with a spooky horse.

The key to understanding almost all of the horse's behavior lies in a single sentence. Let me lead up to it.

"He spooked at nothing at all!" the girl says, brushing the dirt off her jeans and looking bewildered. "We were just trotting along the trail and all of a sudden he jumped sideways and spun around. When I fell off, he ran away. And there wasn't *anything* to be afraid of!"

Later in this chapter we will discuss four things that this kid could have done to keep from getting dumped, but first I'll tell you a story which shows the other side of the coin.

Many years ago in the old board-and-batten farmhouse on our ranch there grew up a young girl named Elizabeth Johns. At the turn of the century she became a school teacher. Her students loved her. They called her "Miss Lizzie."

The school was some fifteen miles away, but she was an excellent horsewoman so she rode—side saddle—back and forth to school. One late afternoon she was riding home from school through the woods when her horse suddenly spooked and jumped sideways. Miss Lizzie hung on and the horse galloped for home, but not before the girl saw a mountain lion land on the ground where she and the horse had been, only a moment before.

Miss Lizzie's grown children told me the story. If her horse hadn't

A horse's instinct when frightened is to run away—but that's why he's survived for us to enjoy him.

spooked at that moment, Miss Lizzie wouldn't have lived to have a family.

Why do horses spook at things and jump and run? Here is the key sentence:

THE HORSE IS AN ANIMAL OF PREY, NOT A PREDATOR.

The first girl couldn't see or hear anything to be afraid of, but the horse had a reason for obeying his most primitive instinct—flight. So did Miss Lizzie's horse. It is this instinct which enabled the horse to survive over millions of years when other species disappeared from the face of the earth. Because of it he outlived mastodons and saber-toothed tigers, so don't knock it! He survived!

The horse has no true weapons for defense. No fangs, no tearing claws, no ripping teeth, no poison to inject, no armor-plated skin. His teeth and his hooves weren't really designed for battle. The horse has but one sure defense against all of the animals that would like to devour him, and that is his speed. Coupled with his speed is a set of senses— hearing, seeing, smelling, and feeling, that act as an alarm system to trigger the horse into action.

If it weren't for his acute senses and great speed, we would have to re-write world history, for the course of history has been determined by armies dependent upon the horse. From the chariots of the Chinese, the Medes, the Persians, and the Egyptians, to the cavalry of Alexander the Great, the Mongolian hordes, the Crusaders, and the Conquistadores of America, the horse in military science not only changed the boundaries of empires but indirectly was responsible for the dissemination of different cultures, sciences, and mathematics.

The horse has a background of almost 58 million years of survival by flight. When you compare this with only 5,000 years of domestication, it should come as no surprise that his nature is still keyed for flight. From his anatomy to his physiology, from his social patterns among other horses to behavior in solitude, the horse is a masterpiece of engineering for survival by flight. His "engineering" is worth studying for that achievement alone, but it is also essential for an understanding of his character.

The horse's vision is very different from ours. His eyes are not located in front, but are set at the side of his head. This gives the horse peripheral vision. He sees not only in front as we do, but his field of vision extends almost to his rear. His vision is monocular as well. Each eye covers a different area and reports a completely different picture to the brain. This means that the horse can get a panoramic view of his surroundings—front, sides, and back—all at the same time without moving!

When his head is up in normal position, his vision around himself is blocked only by his large body. When his head is down to the ground, as in grazing, his vision covers almost a complete circle, blocked only by his four thin legs and a small area directly behind him. Thus he can watch for an enemy while he is grazing without having to interrupt his meal.

Most of the time a horse sees an object with just one eye. He can see it with both eyes only if he is facing it directly—but even then he cannot focus on it as we do. He has to move his head up or down in order to bring the object into focus. This is because the lens of his eye has a fixed shape and cannot be lengthened or shortened as the human lens can. His retina is slanted, and the horse moves his head until the image strikes the place on the retina where the image is in focus. For survival, being able to see all around from a distance was more important than being able to examine something up close.

The horse's ability to watch for predators while he continues to graze is closely related to the way the horse's digestive system works. The horse is constructed with a very small stomach, so he must eat often. A lion or a tiger can gorge himself with a meal and then lie down somewhere to sleep it off—and who's going to bother a sleeping lion? If a horse ate a lot and then lay down to sleep it off, *he'd* be eaten.

Large as the horse is, his stomach only holds about two to four gallons, and it works best when it contains two to two-and-a-half gallons. It is designed for almost constant eating. The stomach secretes gastric juice continuously, whether food is present or not. If he cannot eat often, he is more likely to suffer from indigestion. Food passes through the stomach very rapidly into the intestines where the major part of digestion takes place. A horse kept on good pasture is living more nearly as nature designed him to live—he can graze from time to time around the clock. The grazing horse is the only animal that can take off and run, right after eating, without having a digestive disturbance.

Even a baby horse, called a foal, can run. Within fifteen minutes or so of being born, a foal can be on his feet, wobbly, but walking. In a few more hours, the foal will be able to run fast enough to keep up with the herd.

Another "ready for flight" characteristic is the horse's ability to sleep standing up. He can lock all four legs in place by using an intricate system of ligaments called the "stay apparatus," and thus suspended, fall sound asleep. The stay apparatus ligaments support the horse completely and give the muscles a rest. When startled, the horse can unlock his legs and start running almost immediately.

Occasionally one encounters a horse who does not completely lock his legs for sleeping. For many years we had a Quarter Horse mare who, from time to time, could not get her front legs into position to sleep standing up. She would begin to fall asleep, her head drooping lower and lower. She would stagger a few steps as though drunk and suddenly her front legs would buckle. When her nose hit the ground she would immediately straighten up, look around to see if anyone had noticed, and then stroll around the paddock, clearly pretending she hadn't meant to fall asleep anyway.

After a while she would stand still, close her eyes, and go through the same performance. Once she had so much trouble locking her legs she finally propped herself up against the fence in a corner.

A horse will lie down for short naps and for sunbathing, but never for a long sleep unless he is ill. The weight of his own organs upon his lungs will cause the horse to suffocate if he lies down for too long a time. Nature planned him that way—he wasn't meant to spend much time lying down as he is too vulnerable in that position. When it is nap time in a herd of horses, one or two will always stay awake and be on guard.

A vital part of the horse's alarm system is his hearing. His ears act like radar, and he can pick up sounds beyond human hearing—another horse a half-mile away, or an animal we cannot hear, moving about in the bushes. Out on the trail, one ear is usually steady and pointed straight ahead. The other will be swiveling constantly, like a radar net. His ears take turns. The ear usually works in conjunction with the eye on the same side.

A horse who responds to something suspicious by jumping sideways and running is more likely to survive than the horse who waits around to find out if he should have run.

In case you think that these instincts and abilities are not useful in modern times, consider the two teen-aged girls I knew who were returning home after a long trail ride up a canyon. The girls had miscalculated their time, and it was getting dark. Since horses have excellent night vision, the girls loosened the reins and let the horses find their own way. Near one clump of trees the horses suddenly stopped and refused to follow the path.

Trusting the horses, the girls let them go around the trees and resume the path farther on. As soon as the girls had gotten on the far side of the trees there was a commotion among the branches above the trail. Two men jumped down and started after the girls. Of course the girls put their horses into a gallop and arrived home safely.

The horse's instinct for survival by flight has given him one more valuable characteristic. When a herd was threatened by some danger, it would take off and run for miles until it had outrun the danger. Frequently that flight took the horses far away from their own familiar range where there was adequate food and water. The horse developed a strong homing instinct known as "backtracking" which will enable him to return to his home even though he is many miles away in a strange place. Old-time cowboys can tell you stories of being lost in a blizzard, but by letting the horse have his head, the horse would bring them both safely home.

Now that you are persuaded that all horses are spooky and are likely to bolt, let me assure you that few horses actually do. It is usually the rider who manufactures the problem without realizing it.

What can a kid do to prevent her horse from spooking and dumping her on the ground?

An inexperienced or green rider should not go out on the trail alone, especially on a horse known to be timid. If the kid has no choice but to ride that particular horse, she should find another rider to go with her, one whose horse is calm and trail-wise, who knows that there are no dangers such as a horse-eating chipmunk lying in wait.

Secondly, the green rider must make a supreme effort not to telegraph fear to her horse. When the kid is apprehensive of what might happen, she usually signals this unconsciously to her horse. Her body stiffens, she shortens her reins and takes a death-grip on them, and very likely she grips the saddle with her knees. The horse thinks, good grief, if my person is this scared, I'd better get ready to run. And he does.

Coping with this is not as difficult as you might think. Even if the kid is apprehensive, she can fake it that she's not. She should try to *make* her body relax, and above all *not* grip with her knees. A knee-grip pushes the rider out of the saddle and makes her less secure. The kid can keep the reins loose although ready to shorten them if necessary, touch the horse's withers and scratch them gently where it feels good to him, and sing or talk to her horse. You'd be surprised how quickly the horse will buy that story.

The third thing a kid can do is establish a closer bond with the horse. Every time she cleans his stall or brushes him or cleans his tack where they can see each other, where she can talk to him while she's working, she is cementing this bond. A horse is a herd animal, part of his survival-by-flight syndrome. The herd is his family, and each family has a social order and definite rules which ensure safety for the group.

When you take a horse away from this "family," the substitute family is his rider—his person—your kid. The stronger the bond between them, the less likely the horse will feel apprehension about some strange object when his rider is on board. The horse has a low "panic point," but as he grows to love and trust his rider, his panic point rises to where hardly anything will upset him. He's like a little kid who's afraid of the dark, but when his mother or father is holding his hand, he'll be brave.

The last thing is the most obvious and most time-consuming. The kid must become more experienced in riding! Spending hours in the saddle or on a bareback pad gives the kid the balance necessary so that even if the horse were to jump around, it wouldn't bother the kid.

Michelle's POA Buckshot trusts her so much he walks willingly into a lake to drink.

She will get to know how the horse is feeling and what he is thinking almost as soon as the horse does himself. She can take preventive action when she feels the horse getting upset.

By now you may be wishing that your kid hadn't gone crazy over an animal whose basic instinct is to run away; running away is not what you would term an admirable trait, and kids have a tendency to imitate their friends.

Actually, the horse's basic instinct is survival, and flight alone would not have enabled the horse to survive. For thousands of years in his

59

companionship with man, the horse has demonstrated certain qualities which have captured man's admiration and affection as no other animal has done.

In the next chapter I will discuss some of these qualities. You can decide for yourself if the horse is the kind of friend you'd like your kid to hang around with.

Chapter 7

Getting To Know You

Common terms defined. . . .stages of social development . . . .playfulness. . . .teasing. . . .toys. . . .water play . . . .curiosity. . . .affection. . . .imitative. . . .sense of humor. . . .honesty. . . .non-verbal communication.

When the young British governess in the musical "The King and I," meets her new pupils in Siam, she faces the enormous task of introducing to them a culture that is the complete opposite of their own. The thirty children of the King of Siam bow down to her, and she is expected to teach them of democracy. Where does one begin?

A lilting melody follows and she sings, "Getting to know you, getting to know all about you...Getting to feel free and easy..."

And as they do exactly that, the fear that each feels about the other slowly but surely disappears. I think you will have a similar experience if you are afraid or hesitant about horses but you do make an effort to get to know them. It is worth the effort if you have a horse-crazy kid.

So you'll know what we're talking about, let's first briefly define a few terms. There's a more complete glossary at the back of the book. A baby horse, still nursing, is called a foal. If it is a male, it is also called a colt. If female, a filly. A colt is called a stallion when he is four years old unless he is a Thoroughbred, in which case he must be five years old. A filly at the age of four is called a mare; in Thoroughbreds she must be five.

There are many different kinds or breeds of horses. A pedigreed horse is a horse of any breed with a record of proven ancestry for a certain number of generations. His "registration papers" prove what breed he

Horses are as playful as children — with each other and with things they can use as toys.

is by his pedigree. On the other hand, a Thoroughbred horse is a separate *breed* of horse, not to be confused with the word "purebred." Just as all dogs are animals, but not all animals are dogs, all Thoroughbreds are purebred, but not all purebred horses are Thoroughbreds. We will discuss the different breeds in the chapter, "Four Wheel Drive or Cadillac."

A stallion can be neutered by an operation, after which he is called a gelding (the "g" is hard as in "girl"). Mares can be spayed, but very seldom are. A colt or filly just weaned (from four to six months of age) is called a weanling. A horse between one and two years old is called a yearling.

In spite of their size and appearance, horses are very much like children. Each horse is unique in character and personality. Horses go through stages of development just as children do. Instead of the "terrible two's" of childhood, horses are sweet and affectionate at two, but when they enter the "terrible three's" they can be extremely lively, unpredictable, and have a tendency to argue a lot with their persons. After that there are the "frisky fours." Most horses are not considered mature until they are around six years of age, but some mature sooner while others take a long time to grow up. Some horses seem to be fun-loving all their lives; others are serious and have their lighter side only in brief flashes. And then there are those who are real hellions when young, but grow up to be very dependable. You may know someone like that.

Young horses are quite playful. A band of colts will rough-house with each other, nipping, kicking and running away, rearing and striking, chasing each other, just as a bunch of boys might do. Fillies are equally as playful, but not nearly as rough.

Young horses enjoy playmates—and they don't have to be other horses. We had a newborn filly who thought that our big German shepherd was another horse to play with, and the dog evidently considered the filly a giant frolicsome puppy. They used to play together, taking turns chasing each other in circles in the field. When one tired of the game and walked off, the other quit too.

If a young horse doesn't have someone to play with, he will invent things, just as a child will do. I kept discovering one of the faucets in our campground left on, the water running out of the end of the hose attached to it. I couldn't figure out who did it—and then one day I saw our young filly stroll over to the faucet and with her lips carefully turn on the faucet. When the water started pouring out of the hose, the filly picked up the hose in her teeth and started playing with it, swinging it around to watch the water spray. She played with it for more than three minutes before dropping it and going off to find something else to do.

Sometimes horses like toys to play with. I've known horse owners to tie empty one-gallon plastic milk jugs from the eaves of the horse shelter, or to the fence, for their horses to play with—and the horses do. One person even installed a tether-ball, pole and all, in the middle of the paddock. How that horse loved to push and swing that ball around!

Before the cross-fencing was put around our house, the horses in the pasture could come up and peer in our windows to see what we were doing. If they thought we were late for feeding time, they would begin zinging their teeth on the window screens for attention.

The young filly (the same one who turned on the water faucet) one day discovered the doormat by the front door, and trotted off with it in her mouth, shaking it up and down and back and forth, delighted with her new toy. If I had chased after her, she would have run away with it. I went outside and pretended to be busy with something. After a while she dropped the doormat in the field and went off. I strolled in the direction of the doormat—but she had been watching me. Like a flash she came galloping over to grab it before I could pick it up. I had to pretend that I wasn't after the doormat at all. A half an hour passed before I could reclaim the doormat.

We had a colt who enjoyed teasing other horses. When he had teased another horse long enough for the annoyed horse to want to do something about it, the colt would run and hide behind his mother and act as though he had been there a long time.

Once when he had run and hid and nothing happened, he peeked out from behind his mother to discover that the horse he was teasing had decided to ignore him. A minute later the colt dashed out from behind his mother, ran right across in front of his victim, kicked up his heels at that horse's nose as he went by, and hid behind a horse on the other side of the herd. Does that remind you of anyone you know?

Like children, some horses enjoy playing in water. I've seen them swing their heads back and forth in the water trough, splashing the water all around before they got down to business to drink. One mare used to submerge her head almost to her eyes and blow bubbles, lift her head out, take a big breath, and duck her head again to blow more bubbles.

Some horses love to swim, and others never get the hang of it and could easily drown. I knew one horse who got all excited when he was ridden bareback to a local lake to play. The horse's idea of playing in the lake was splashing. He liked to trot merrily in and out of the water, lifting his feet up as high as he could and bringing them down to see how big a splash he could make. As soon as he got to a depth where he couldn't splash, he'd turn around and splash back out while his kid laughed and shouted.

Horses are very curious, and like children, it seems that the more intelligent the horse, the more curious he is.

This spring we turned out our five-horse-power mower (five horses) in the campground to mow the grass for us. The newest horse, Flyer, recently off the race-track, was enchanted with the playground equipment. He ran the teeter-totter up and down with his nose, swung the swings, and especially enjoyed the glider, pushing it back and forth and following it with his head as though he were at a tennis match. He didn't begin grazing until he was perfectly satisfied with the way everything worked. This horse is extremely intelligent and enjoys his lessons.

Curiosity is a trait which can be used in making friends with a timid horse. I had gone into a paddock to try to catch a big filly that had not been handled very much, and she wasn't about to let me get near her. I finally knelt down in the middle of the paddock (a non-threatening position because the person is then shorter than the horse) and started rubbing my hands together. The filly stopped galloping around the paddock and step by step approached me, head down and studying my hands. She finally got close enough to be able to sniff my hands, then my hair, and then my face. I don't think she'd ever had the chance to check out a human before.

It was February and cold; when she sniffed my glasses they steamed up, and instantly she jumped and took off. I smothered a laugh and kept on with what I was doing. She slowly returned to me, leaned forward, and deliberately blew on my glasses. When they steamed up again she jumped, but held her ground.

After that it was a game, and when I started to blow into her nostrils, she blew right back and obviously enjoyed it. Blowing in each other's nostrils is the way horses greet each other. In a short while I was stroking her face, and soon after that I slipped a rope over her neck. She never fought at all but followed me as though I were a long-lost friend.

Most horses are affectionate, especially if they have been brought up in an affectionate "household."

One of our colts was so affectionate that if he had been a human he would have held hands with you. Since he couldn't hold your hand, he decided the next best thing was to walk along with you with his head over your shoulder and his face near yours. That could be disconcerting if you were not used to horses. This colt always wanted to help you with whatever you were doing—he wanted to hold the hammer, or else hold the nails, and if you didn't give him something to do, he would walk off with a tool you were about to use so you would have to go after him.

Horses, like children, are imitative. If an older horse has a bad habit or two, it won't be long before a young horse stabled near him will pick up those same bad habits. A horse who enjoys chewing his fence will very shortly have the horses near him chewing their fences, too. A horse who is a weaver, swaying back and forth as he stands at the stall door, will soon have some of the other horses weaving also. Most of these bad habits or "vices" originate from intense boredom on the part of horses not given enough freedom outside their stalls. Such vices are common among race horses.

Since horses imitate each other, a good way to educate a young horse is to put him with an older horse who has those qualities you want the younger horse to develop.

We had had a young colt gelded, and during his recovery we kept him in a paddock with straw for bedding. The day the soiled straw was to be removed by a tractor with a skip loader, we moved the colt to an adjoining small paddock occupied by an older, very calm and wise horse. The tractor bucket scooped up the straw, the bucket was lifted up, and unfortunately was swung out over the two horses in the adjoining paddock. The colt was so terrified he nearly turned himself inside out and tried to jump over the five-foot fence.

The older horse, however, looked up at the bucket going overhead, clearly said to himself something like, "Well, whaddyaknow, a bucket going overhead," and went back to eating his hay. The frightened colt stared at his big friend, looked up at the bucket, back at his friend, and stepped up to the manger and went on eating, too. No amount of explaining to the colt could have been more effective than the behavior of the big horse. When the colt grew up, he was just as cool and laid-back as the older horse. Both, incidentally, were Thoroughbreds, a breed reputedly high-strung.

Horses, especially Arabians, can exhibit a strong sense of humor. By invitation, I stopped one day at the home of a new friend to meet her horse, an elderly Arabian mare who was retired along with her elderly owner. The mare came up to be patted. I set my hand-bag on the ground and reached up to pat the mare. The mare grabbed my hand-bag by the handles and dashed off for about twenty feet, whirled, and stood there with the hand-bag dangling from her mouth, looking for all the world like a mischievous child. Her owner said in a scolding voice, "You naughty girl. You bring that right back." The mare reluctantly, step by step, walked forward to me and put the hand-bag at my feet.

Horses are good at figuring out how to get what they want. A friend of ours kept his Arabian trail horse in a large paddock with a washtub in one corner for water. Our friend filled the tub from a hose which was left looped over the fence near the tub. Whenever the horse wanted more water in his tub, he would pick up the hose in his teeth and bang the nozzle against the tub until someone came out of the house to turn on the faucet.

One of the most admirable traits of the horse is his honesty. Horses are very straightforward. Horses use non-verbal communication, and they never try to hide their feelings. A horse never lies to you, or says one thing to your face and something else behind your back.

A horse who was brought in to our stable had apparently been mistreated by men. One man tried unsuccessfully to saddle him. Four men finally got the horse into the horsewash rack where they tried to put a saddle on him, but the horse kicked apart the whole rack. The men gave up on him, put him back in his stall, and vowed to get rid of him.

Shortly afterward, a fourteen-year-old girl showed up for her lesson, and she heard the story of the new horse. She felt sorry for him and went to his stall to give him some carrots and talk to him. He was so eager and affectionate with her that she led him out and decided to try to ride him. She saddled and bridled him with no difficulty, and rode him in her lesson. Eventually she bought him and rode him for years. But the horse never would let a man saddle him. The horse was completely honest in telling people how he felt.

Some of the horse's non-verbal communication is very obvious even to a non-horse person. He tenses when he's apprehensive; he trembles when he's scared; he breaks into a sweat when he gets excited; his pulse and respiration shoot up when he's under stress. His body sags when he's tired. He utters a big sigh when he's relaxing. But there's a lot more to it than that. Skillful reading of the horse's non-verbal communication means studying the whole horse over a long period of time. Some good books have been written on this fascinating subject.

If you find people interesting to watch, you will probably enjoy watching horses, especially when there is a group of them together. When you know how to read their non-verbal communication, their "conversation" can be as entertaining as people at a party.

Some persons say that horses do not experience emotions like humans, but in many cases I have seen horses *act* as though they do. Actions speak louder than words. As you read the next chapter, you be the judge.

Chapter 8

Getting To Know You Better

Demonstrating emotions—joy, friendship, grief, jealousy, responsibility, regret, fairness, reasoning, love.

Any observant person who is with horses a great deal soon realizes that horses exhibit a wide range of emotions. These emotions certainly seem to correspond very closely with our own.

If you were in a strange place and were suddenly to meet a friend of yours whom you hadn't seen or heard of for a number of years, wouldn't you be excited about it?

My horse, a big chestnut, had been a stablemate with a palomino mare named Taffy for several years. Eventually the horses went their separate ways. About three years later, when my horse was in an entirely different barn, I learned that Taffy was about to move into the same stable. Her owner and I wondered if the horses would remember each other. A few days later we found out.

I had dismounted and was leading my horse as I entered the long aisle of the main barn in which twelve or so stalls lined the aisle on each side. Coming in from bright sunlight to the darkened barn, I was walking slowly until my eyes adjusted. I did see a horse enter the barn aisle at the other end, silhouetted briefly in the sunlight. Three steps later my horse abruptly stopped and stiffened, then craned his neck forward, sniffing. Suddenly he nickered and began pulling me forward in the aisle, hastening to the horse walking toward us.

It was Taffy, the palomino mare, and as the two horses met in the center of the barn, both arched their necks, dropped their heads, and touched their faces together, nickering very softly down deep. No one could possibly doubt the joy in the reunion of the two.

It's nice to know that with horses, friends really count. Horses are very sociable; the few that are anti-social have usually been made that way by humans. They are a herd animal, surviving because together they have more resources for detecting danger and for protecting their young.

If a horse is lacking another horse for a companion, he will form a friendship with another species. Dogs, cats, goats, and ponies, all can become best buddies with a horse and keep him from being lonely. One of our horses, formerly on the racetrack, must have had a cat for a companion in his stall. Whenever one of our cats comes near, the horse puts his head down to the ground and holds still so the cat can rub himself back and forth against the horse's face. The horse seems to enjoy it as much as the cat.

The famous Thoroughbred stakes racer, Stymie, had as a friend a nondescript old hen. Whenever Stymie was in his stall, the hen would roost on his back.

Horses not only develop strong attachments to friends, they apparently can grieve at their loss. This was demonstrated by the great Thoroughbred racehorse, Exterminator.

He was not a good-looking Thoroughbred. He was tall, angular, and boney, a natural for the nickname Bones. As he grew older he was Old Bones. In spite of his appearance he was a great favorite with the crowds because of his personality. He was easy to handle in the stables and saddling area. He was even a gentleman going to the post.

While other horses were nervous and jittery before a race, Old Bones would stroll leisurely to the starting line. There he would stand quietly with his ears lopped, waiting for the signal. But when the race started, it was a different story. Old Bones would get into gear in back of the pack and start running. He seemed to enjoy coming from behind and, in keeping with his name, exterminate his competition. He ran a total of 100 races of which he won 50, placed second 17 times, and third 17 times.

His career came to an end at the age of nine when he suffered a leg injury on the track and was honorably retired. But after years of excitement from racing, crowds, applause, and trips to the winner's circle, Old Bones didn't take kindly to the change. Horses, like some people, can find retirement difficult. Exterminator became quite unruly and for the first time in his life was difficult to handle.

Then a stablehand suggested a pony as a companion. The pony introduced was so small he could walk underneath the big bony Thoroughbred. Named Peanuts, the pony and Old Bones became the best of friends, and very shortly the old racehorse regained his good-natured disposition.

Horses need friendship—with each other, with other animals, or with humans.

Some years later the pony died of colic. When the body was removed, the racehorse became frantic and refused to eat. Who knows what might have become of the big horse had not one of the stablehands suggested that the dead pony be put back in the stall. All that night Exterminator lay with his head across the dead pony's form. He finally seemed to realize that his little friend was gone, and in the morning he let the men take the pony away.

If the big horse wasn't grieving, what was it?

Some time later another pony, Peanuts II, was introduced. He became the best friend of Old Bones until the racehorse himself died of natural causes at the age of 30. When Peanuts II died shortly afterward, he was buried beside the great racehorse.

If your kid had a best friend, and her best friend suddenly became interested in someone else, wouldn't your kid be jealous, and try to win back her friend?

Most horsemen have had the occasion to ride a different horse while their own horse stayed in his stall. Sometimes the owner's horse doesn't seem to care, but other times a horse will throw a fit. I remember trying out a new horse that had come into our stable. My own horse paid little attention until I saddled the newcomer and rode him past my horse's paddock.

My horse was furious and lunged at the stranger with teeth bared. All the time I was riding, my horse raced around in his paddock and kicked and yelled at the top of his lungs just like a kid throwing a temper tantrum. When I put away the visiting horse and got my own horse out, he was still mad at me. He laid his ears back and rolled his eyes and sulked for half an hour after I mounted him. I kept talking nicely to him as I rode, trying to sound cheerful and matter-of-fact, and after a while he settled down.

The next day when I took him out we had a wonderful ride together. He was eager to obey and responded quickly to every command. Not only that, but he performed more brilliantly than he ever had before.

The message he gave me was clearly, "Please don't ever look at another horse. See what a good horse I am!"

As a parent, you may be busy with your own activities until some crisis threatens your family. Immediately your family takes first priority. We saw this happen among our herd of horses who normally graze over many acres. They have a well-established social order. They used to take orders from the lead mare, who got her orders from the lead gelding, a Thoroughbred. When the lead mare became inactive from arthritis, she completely relinquished her authority to the gelding.

This winter, the lead gelding suffered a deep cut above the hoof on his left hind leg. We had to shut him up in a sheltered paddock so we could treat his foot and keep him from running around. He didn't seem to mind being shut up because he was lame, and besides, the rest of the herd was on the other side of the fence and could talk to him.

But then a snowstorm struck, and as the snow filled the air the Thoroughbred went into a frenzy in his paddock, rearing and striking and charging about. He is well acquainted with snow and enjoys playing in it, so it wasn't the snow that upset him. We figured it was his being unable to look after his family! We had to let him out to keep him from further injuring his leg. He dashed out of the paddock and rounded up his family and eventually got them all into the barn, where he quieted down and was his normal self.

People can live through an unpleasant situation, put it out of their minds, and eventually think it completely forgotten. But if some incident triggers that memory, it's possible for a person to react badly as though the unpleasant situation were still there.

I knew of a horse whose owner was having marital problems. The man took out his anger and frustration on his horse, using any excuse for beating the horse and jerking him around. The horse retaliated by bucking the man off at least once a week. If the horse was lucky, it was twice a week. Eventually the horse was sold and came into our barn. I rode the horse over a period of several years, and during that time he never tried to buck—except once, and the circumstances were unusual.

I was riding the horse in a big arena when he suddenly became very upset, trembling and throwing his head. Then without warning he unloaded me. As I flew through the air, I heard a man laugh. When I got up I looked around to see the horse's former owner riding by on another horse. "I see he hasn't changed any," said the man.

But what of the horse? He should have gone tearing off around the ring, bucking, but instead he stood still with his head down and his whole body shaking. It seemed to me he realized that he had bucked off the wrong person and was sorry. I walked up to him and put my arms around his neck and he leaned against me with a big sigh. He never bucked again as long as I rode him.

I've read several scientific articles in which the authors maintained that horses are not able to reason. They probably hadn't been around horses very much. I'd like to draw their attention to the day I had a confrontation with our red dun mare.

Some years ago where we lived I used to trailer two horses to a distant riding ring for schooling. I always rode the younger more difficult horse first, a spirited Thoroughbred, and then if I had strength left I'd ride the other horse.

The other horse, a quiet red dun Quarter Horse mare, tried to tell me in various ways that she didn't like always being second choice, but I wouldn't listen. While I was riding dressage on the Thoroughbred, the mare would nibble cautiously on the wooden markers I used as letters. As soon as I started toward her to spank her, she would move away and look innocent as though to say, "Who, me? I wasn't doing anything." I couldn't spank her then because she had stopped, so I had to go on with my riding.

One day as I was unloading the horses from the trailer it occurred to me that the red dun had trained *me* very well. She knew just when to nibble the markers to get my attention, and how to keep from getting spanked. I made up my mind that today was the day things would be different.

She began nibbling on the middle marker as I rode down the long side of the dressage "arena," but this time I pretended I didn't see her. I watched from the corner of my eye. She stopped nibbling, evidently puzzled, but didn't move away, and then slowly began to nibble again.

When I was opposite the mare, I whapped her on the rump with the end of my dressage whip. She gave me a look of pained surprise, whirled, and galloped off toward the gate.

Now this mare was extremely clever at opening all kinds of locks and gates, and it occurred to me she might try to open the arena gate and take off. I halted and watched with growing concern, ready to gallop to the gate if she should start working on the latch.

She didn't go to the gate, but to the fence panel next to the gate, where I hung my sweatshirt. I always hung my sweatshirt there, and never before had she paid any attention to it. But this time she galloped up to my sweatshirt, snatched it off the fence, and shook it and shook it and shook it. The dust rose around her in a cloud as the sweatshirt hit first the ground and then her rump as she tossed her head up and down. Then she dropped the sweatshirt on the ground and walked across it and stood there looking at me.

What could I say? I not only hadn't listened to her; I had added insult to injury. She was desperate. She wouldn't do anything to hurt me, so she used my sweatshirt to get her message across. I finally got it.

After that I always alternated my first ride between the two horses. She was a happier horse; I could tell by the way she performed. And she never again nibbled on the markers.

Perhaps you have concluded as I have that horses act a lot like people. We don't need to attribute human emotions to them—we can readily identify with their own emotions.

As well as sensitivity, there are many other admirable qualities in a horse. Numerous horse stories illustrate great courage, determination, and generosity. There was the winning English race horse, Humorist, who, it was discovered after his death, had only one lung. There was Justin Morgan, the sturdy little bay horse from Vermont who out-pulled, out-walked, out-trotted, and out-ran every four-legged competitor put up against him. There was the jumper, Do Right, who carried Dennis Murphy to victory in the Nations Cup in the puissance class in Madison Square Gardens when Do Right went clean over the biggest fence he had ever taken—a height of 7'1". There was the Thoroughbred Black Gold, a winner on the track except for his last race, when one of his forelegs snapped in the homestretch and he still tried on three legs to reach the wire first. There was Flora Temple, known as the "little cricket," a small bay mare with a bobbed tail who responded to the outstanding horses put up against her by breaking one trotting record after another, and in 103 races over eleven racing seasons, lost only 17 races. There was Jay Trump, who sliced himself open on a lamp post when he jumped the infield rail in his first race and was saved from the track vet's bullet by his dedicated owner—surviving to win not only the triple crown of steeplechasing in the United States, but the English Grand National as well. There was Might Tango, the gallant grey horse who gave all he could to Bruce Davidson in the cross-country course of the Three-Day World Championships in Lexington, Kentucky, collapsing as he came off the course—and willingly the next day entered the stadium jumping ring to bring home the Gold Medal for the U.S. Equestrian Team.

Famous military leaders have felt they owed so much of their success to their horses that military honors have been heaped upon the horses after their death.

What is there in the make-up of the horse that enables him to carry out these feats? Over and over again horses demonstrate a capacity for love and affection, loyalty, generosity, fairness, and honesty. No wonder your kid is horse-crazy. Your kid could do lots worse than relate to a friend with those qualities.

I hope that your reading has given you a better idea of what to expect from a horse. The next chapter will tell you what you should expect from your kid. It is important for her welfare as well as for your own peace of mind.

Chapter 9

The First Rules Of Safety First

*Safety measures not taught....catching....leading
....through gates....tying....working around horse
....watching feet....checking stirrups and girth....
mounting....warm-up....dismounting.*

Now that I've pointed out to you many ways in which horses are like children, let me tell you that in many other ways horses are NOT like children, and the difference between the two is crucial for your kid's safety.

Frequently an instructor does not *make* time to teach the very first rules of safety first to his students. Some times he even takes for granted that the students will be safety conscious. He is being paid to teach the kid to ride—but here are some safety measures that your kid should know. Many of these are taught in stable management by the U.S. Pony Club, and our U.S. Equestrian Team follows them. They are valid whether your kid is riding English or Western. You should see that your kid follows them.

Anyone working with horses should remember the "three ly's." That person should move *slowly*, speak *softly*, and touch *gently*. The kid should always approach the horse at his shoulder, not from his rear or his front, talking to the horse as she approaches so he knows she is there. A startled or surprised horse is a scared horse, and a scared horse can do damage without meaning to.

When anyone is leading a horse with a rope, the rope must *never* be coiled around the hand or over the arm. It must be looped back and forth or "figure-eighted." This is essential to prevent a serious deep cut or the kid being dragged as the rope tightens on hand or arm if something should suddenly make the horse jump and pull away.

Usually a horse for a riding lesson is already tacked up, or is in a stall where the kid can get him. Once in a while the school horses will be in a group in a corral and the kid has to catch the horse herself. For various reasons, the horse may decide he does not want to be caught, and he hurries away when he sees the kid approaching with a halter in hand. Tell your kid not to chase the horse, for the horse will then

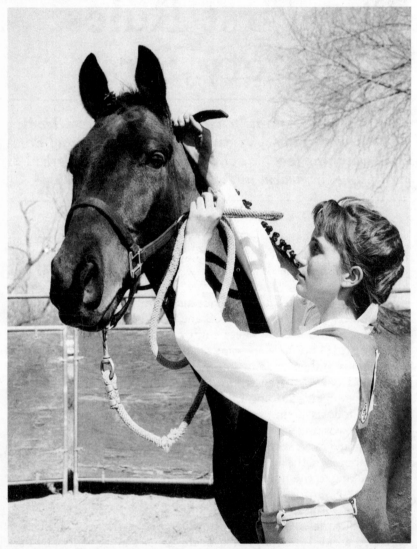

Festus stands willingly while Caroline fastens the halter properly.

think it is a game and prolong the action. The kid should simply follow the horse leisurely, talking to the horse in the meantime, and holding out a tidbit such as a piece of carrot. Almost always the horse will eventually give up and stand still for the reward. If the horse is very difficult to catch, it's not the right horse for a kid and you'd better see that she takes lessons on some other horse or at a different stables.

The common way of catching a horse is to throw a rope over the horse's neck and then put the halter on. One word of caution. A horse occasionally will spin and leave when he feels a hand or rope going *over* his neck. Putting the noseband of the halter on first avoids this problem. This way is also easier for a short person with a tall horse.

The kid should hold the halter in both hands in the position for putting it on the horse and at the same time hold the end of the tie rope in her left hand. Give the horse a tidbit, and while he is munching, slip the noseband over the horse's nose. Instead of backing out, most horses think they are caught fair and square and will stand. Have the kid's right hand reach under the horse's neck, feel for the loose end of the halter's neck-piece, and flip it up on the far side of the neck so it crosses the top of the neck and comes down on the near side where the kid is standing. Then the kid can grab the end of it and finish buckling the halter. In time the kid can omit the tidbit.

If the horse is small enough or the kid big enough, after the noseband has been slid over the horse's nose, it's okay for the kid to reach over the horse's neck and grab the neck-piece. Having the noseband on first keeps the horse from freaking out and charging off.

Don't expect the horse to try to avoid stepping on the kid. The horse has four feet of his own to think about, and that's enough. It's entirely up to your kid to keep her own two feet out from under his four. This is why bare feet and sandals are a no no around horses. If he should put his foot on her toes, she should kick the offending leg with her other foot or hit him as hard as she can to get him off. Once he's off, the horse does *not* merit punishment because your kid's feet were not his responsibility.

The safest way to lead a horse is to stand on the horse's left side (called the near side) about opposite his left shoulder. The kid should face the same direction as the horse, with the kid's right hand holding the lead rope about six inches below where the lead rope snaps on to the halter. The kid's left hand holds the end of the lead rope in a figure eight, not coiled around her hand. She can give the horse a little tug forward with the right hand and say, "Walk," and start walking. She should *never walk in front of the horse* because he can easily step on her by mistake. She should walk beside his left shoulder. The kid's right elbow is then close to the horse's neck and can be used to push the horse away if he starts to crowd.

To stop the horse, the kid should give a little tug backward on the lead rope and say "Ho," or "Whoa." As soon as the horse obeys, she should give him a pat and say, "Good boy" (or good girl, as the case may be). The horse can't read your kid's mind, and the reward tells him that's what the kid wanted him to do. Horses, like kids, would rather be rewarded than scolded.

When the kid leads her horse in and out of a stall or a paddock, it is very important for the kid to close the gate behind her without letting go of the lead rope *or* the gate. The horse will learn very quickly to expect to be turned around and go back to the gate each time. This simple procedure prevents the gate from swinging and hitting the horse, or the kid, or somebody else that was just going by. It also prevents the horse from suddenly bolting out the gate and knocking down the kid if something should spook him. Last of all, when your kid is trail riding and wants to open or close a gate without dismounting, the horse has already been trained to approach the gate correctly.

Closing the paddock gate behind the kid helps stable safety in one more way. I have known horses who figure out the catch on the paddock, and let themselves out to play. I have never known a horse to turn around and close his own gate behind him, though a friend of ours has two remarkable horses that do. If everyone at the stable closes the gate behind them, and someone finds an empty paddock with an open gate, they will know that almost always the horse is loose on his own and someone can start looking for him.

A vital safety measure is the knot with which the horse is tied. He must *always* be tied with a quick-release knot. If he is not tied that way and something frightens him so that he pulls back with all his weight on the lead-rope (this is called "laying-back"), the only way you can release the horse is to take a knife and cut the rope. Not only is this expensive, but if the horse is injured and must be released quickly, finding a knife can take too long a time. With a properly tied quick-release knot, no matter how hard the horse is pulling back, a strong pull on the loose end of the lead-rope will release him. (See the drawing.) To prevent a horse from untying himself, after tying the knot, slip the free end of the rope through the loop.

When a horse is to be tied to something, the something must always be an immovable object. You would be astonished at the size and weight of immovable objects that become movable when a horse tied to them is frightened and tries to break loose. A horse has incredible strength when he uses his whole weight with leverage. Fence posts can be broken like match sticks, a car door can be ripped off, and medium-size trees uprooted. A horse tied to a horse trailer can tip over the trailer if it is not hitched to a vehicle. I once tied a horse to the metal ring imbedded in a huge brick backyard barbecue. When something frighten-

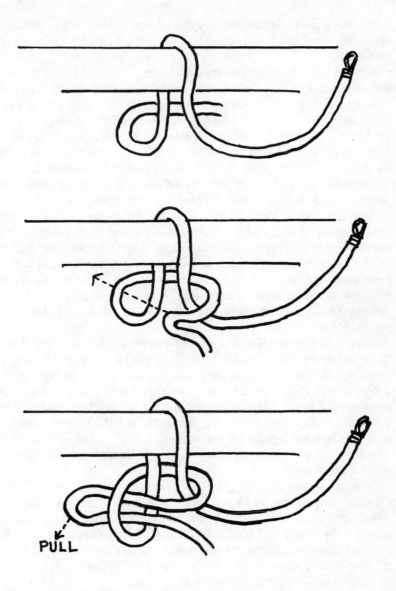

The quick-release knot—the only safe way to tie a horse. Your kid should practice this until it is easy for her.

ed the horse, he pulled the brick barbecue out of the ground and dragged it several feet. I couldn't blame the horse—he didn't tie himself to the barbecue.

When your kid is working around a horse, she should not only watch her own feet, but keep the horse informed as to where she is. The horse that kicks a person on purpose is extremely rare and you certainly shouldn't have your kid working with a horse like that. If the kid talks or whistles or sings as she works around the horse she is much less likely to get hurt. When she walks behind the horse she doesn't need to give him a wide berth. In fact, if she puts her hand on his rump as she walks behind him, the horse will usually try not to kick at the fly on his tummy until the kid is out of the way.

At many stables the school horses will be gotten ready for riding by grooms, and all the kid has to do is adjust the length of the stirrup leathers for her own legs, and mount. In English riding, a general rule of thumb is that the leathers are about right when the kid can put her finger tips on the bump of the saddle where the stirrup leather is attached, and stretching her arm, the stirrup iron will just fit under her arm pit. In Western riding the stirrup should be a little longer than for English.

There's one other thing she should *always* do, no matter how good the grooms are. She should check the girth or cinch to be sure it is tight. It's like packing your own parachute if you're going to jump.

No human is comfortable with a belt that is too tight; horses don't like too-tight girths. Mares are more sensitive about their tummies than geldings. If the rider cinches up the girth as tight as she can at the start, the horse will probably learn in self defense to take a deep breath which he can let out later. The horse is more comfortable, but the girth will be too loose.

To avoid such a problem, the rider should fasten the cinch lightly, do something else for a half-minute or so, go back and tighten the cinch a little bit more, do something else, and tighten again. Horses seldom take a deep breath and hold it if this method is followed. It is so easy for the rider to take her time and have a happy horse, so why not do it? And fifteen minutes after mounting, the girth or cinch should be checked again.

A black mare came into our barn who swung her head and tried to bite me the instant I put my hand on the girth. Obviously her former owner had used the "oof" method of cinching up. When the rider starts tightening the cinch and the horse takes a breath or "blows up," the rider lifts his knee and jabs the horse in the stomach as hard as possible. The horse goes "oof" and lets out the air, and the rider instantly tightenes the cinch. When cinched this way, the horse often develops the habit of biting the person who is saddling him. I can hardly blame the horse, but a horse that bites is undesirable. Encourage your kid to take her time, be safe, and still have a happy horse.

What did I do about the black mare? I stepped back so she couldn't reach me and fastened the girth very loosely, then patted her and gave her a slice of carrot. In a little while I tightened the girth ever so slightly, patted her and gave her another slice. I kept this up until the girth was properly adjusted. It took me fifteen minutes, but it was worth it. The next day it took only ten minutes. By the end of the week the mare was looking forward to having the saddle put on, and she didn't try again to bite. When she learned that the girth was not going to hurt her, I didn't have to give her any more carrots.

Mounting and dismounting are the two times when people most often get hurt by a horse because they don't take the simplest of precautions.

Horses are usually mounted from the horse's left side, called the near side. In the Middle Ages, only men of high rank rode horses, and they carried swords. The scabbard hung on the left so the sword could be drawn by the right hand. The presence of the scabbard made it necessary to mount the horse on his left side. A lot of our customs in riding date back to the age of chivalry. Mounting from the left or near side is one of those customs. A well-trained horse, however, especially a cow pony, can be mounted from either side equally well.

Your kid's horse should be trained to stand still when the kid gets on. The cowboy that leaps onto a moving horse is one who has been riding for years and he knows what he's doing. If the horse thinks that putting one foot in the stirrup is the signal to move out, the kid can easily be dumped on the ground. A rider on his way to the ground with one foot still in the stirrup is in BIG trouble.

When your kid mounts, her left hand should hold both reins and also the horse's mane. If her horse has a tendency to start off while she is mounting, she should shorten the reins until the horse can feel the contact. If he continues to start off, she may be riding the wrong kind of horse for a beginner. If she has no choice in horses, someone should stand on the far (right) side of the horse and hold the cheek piece of the bridle (not the reins) until she is safely on top.

Don't let your kid get in the habit of mounting and galloping away. She may think it makes her look like a great rider, but she is actually showing her ignorance. If the horse has been standing in his paddock or stall, he needs to be warmed up before vigorous exercise. Here's why:

Have your kid lift up one of the horse's feet so you can see the bottom of it. You'll notice a v-shaped wedge in the center of the hoof. This is called the frog. The frog acts like treads on the bottom of hiking shoes—it's a device that reduces concussion and helps the horse stop quickly.

Even more important, the frog helps activate a secondary "heart" in the horse's foot. The horse's heart has to pump his blood down into his long thin legs. To get the blood back up again isn't easy, especially when the horse is exercising. Nature very cleverly put a wedge on each hoof so that when the hoof touches the ground, the pressure helps return the blood back to the heart. If the horse has been standing around, he needs to be walked for ten or fifteen minutes before exercising to allow the circulatory system in his feet to get warmed up.

When the movie cowboy runs to his horse at the tie rail, jumps on, and gallops away, you may be sure he had already warmed up his horse before tying him to the rail.

Your kid's horse should also be made to stand still when your kid dismounts. With an English saddle, the safest way is to have your kid kick *both feet out of the stirrups*. She should put both hands on the pommel (the front) of the saddle, lean forward and put her weight on them, extend the right leg straight and swing it over the horse's back until both legs are together, then slide down to the ground.

Western riders always swing their right leg over the horse's rump and then step down, leaving the left foot in the stirrup until the right foot is on the ground. This is easy for a grown man riding a small cow pony. When your kid is an experienced rider and is tall enough to step down gracefully, she can do that too. In the meantime, I suggest your kid put her hands on the fork of the saddle, put her weight on them, and swing the right foot over the horse's back. When she has both feet together on the left side, the left foot still in the stirrup, she can then let go the left stirrup and drop down to the ground with both feet.

Dropping both stirrups prevents getting a foot caught and getting dumped or dragged. It also lets a rider dismount safely from a moving horse in an emergency. Your kid can learn that later.

Sooner or later, the day will arrive when your kid has been counting on an exciting lesson on her favorite school horse only to discover that someone else is riding that horse. Be prepared for stormy weather and wailing from your kid that *she needs her own horse.*

It's very unlikely that your kid will be able to think of any reasons why she shouldn't have her own horse. And if she could, I doubt if she would tell you about them. It's up to you, the parent, to learn both the advantages and disadvantages of ownership and weigh them well before you consider that step. In the next chapter I'll point out to you some of the pros and cons.

Chapter 10

The Good News And The Bad News

Horse costs little to acquire . . . . a lot to maintain . . . .
constant care and constant expense . . . . feed . . . . stabling
. . . . horseshoeing . . . . veterinary care . . . . equipment
. . . . clothing . . . . instruction . . . . activities . . . .
insurance . . . . why you shouldn't buy a horse . . . .
alternatives—books, work, vaulting.

Whether your kid takes lessons in a large class or with private instruction, she will develop a preference for one or two of the horses she is assigned to ride. As she gets to know that horse well, she discovers that the horse obeys her more quickly. Each is learning the other's cues, and a bond of mutual trust and affection develops between them.

That's when your kid begins to realize the true value of having her own horse. She and the horse are establishing a relationship which increases their pleasure in riding. Wanting a horse because of the rewarding relationship is different from wanting a horse for convenience, or because her friends have horses, or because of a romantic dream.

Before your kid gets completely sold on the idea of owning a horse, I would like to give you some good news and bad news of horse ownership.

The good news is that the purchase price of a horse does not have to be high. In fact, horses are occasionally available with no price tag at all—they are free, perhaps delivered to your door.

Don't be fooled by "how cheap" your kid can get a horse. Frequently horses that are free or have a low price tag have vices or lack of training that make them difficult to handle on the ground or dangerous to ride. That's definitely not the kind of horse you want your kid to have.

However, there are some horses who can no longer compete on the show circuit because of some lameness problem which requires special attention. The owners are often glad to find a good home for these horses, with no price tag. A *known* lameness is not so bad if the horse on medication is safe and servicably sound for the kid's intended purpose. A veterinarian is best equipped to make that decision. Some of these horses make ideal mounts for children.

Horses do come in all prices, and you don't have to break the bank to get your kid started with a horse. You could, if you wish, pay a fortune for a horse, but that is not a wise investment to make for a novice rider.

The bad news of owning a horse is:

(1) the cost of maintaining a horse is a substantial amount and must be paid, month in and month out, even if he is not being ridden at all.

(2) a horse requires constant care, no matter how much or little the horse is ridden.

Let's first discuss cost.

Prices for products and services fluctuate a great deal from year to year and in different locations. Rather than list the cost of hay or horseshoeing in various parts of the country at the time of this writing, I suggest you make inquiry of a knowledgeable horseman, your local stables, feed stores, and tack stores to learn the going prices in your area of each of the following expenses. Then you can calculate how much of a financial burden a horse will place on your family.

Here is a list of the horse-owner's expenses:

Feed. The horse must be given enough feed to keep him in good condition, according to his type and the amount of exercise he gets. One horse consumes between three and four tons of hay in one year, plus supplements. The cost of feed is higher in winter than in summer.

Stabling. Your kid isn't going to keep the horse in her room (although she might like to) so she must have a good place to keep him, and a good place to ride him. This means in a boarding stable or in someone's back yard, perhaps your own. Boarding stables are more expensive than maintaining a horse at home, but usually the stables take good care of horses and, an important factor, have lessons available. If the horse is kept at your own home, you will need a place to store the feed as well as the tack.

Horseshoeing or trimming. A horse's hooves grow constantly, like your fingernails. A horse needs to have a farrier or horseshoer check his feet every six to eight weeks. Horseshoes are a necessary evil since man took over the care of the horse. Horseshoes are meant to protect the bottom of the horse's feet and keep them from wearing down faster than they can grow out.

Veterinary care. Veterinary expense includes regular vaccinations against certain diseases, worming for internal parasites on a regular basis, and care of the teeth. There are always emergencies, when the horse gets hurt or goes lame or seems to be sick. Murphy's Law applies here—the horse will need the vet when you can afford it the least. Find out the name of several good veterinarians and their charge for house (barn) calls.

Equipment and horse clothing. The cost of riding equipment and tack for the horse varies according to the quality, from "adequate" to "top of the line." This includes halters and lead ropes, bridles, saddles, grooming tools, buckets, blankets, etc., and a place to store them.

Rider clothing. Clothing for the rider can be inexpensive or items of luxury, but boots or hard-soled shoes have to be at the top of the list. An AHSA approved helmet is preferred for riding, and a *must* for any kind of jumping. As for the rest, from blue jeans to custom-tailored breeches, there is a world of choices.

Instruction. If your kid does acquire a horse, it is highly desirable for her to continue instruction. Just as you wouldn't get a piano or violin for your kid without arranging for lessons, she should not be expected to teach herself to handle the new horse.

Activities and recreation. Your expenses will increase if your kid wants to take part in horse shows, horse sports, or in gymkhanas (playdays on horseback). Entry fees and equipment add up in a hurry. Sometimes trailering fees have to be included.

Insurance. Rates at this writing are astronomical. Most people don't think about equine insurance unless they are dealing with very expensive horses, but the definition of "expensive" depends upon your personal financial situation. If your horse's value is such that you cannot afford the loss, you might consider insuring the horse.

It is definitely wise to have some kind of personal liability insurance so that if your kid's horse kicks someone causing injury, your insurance will pay for it. Most home owners' policies provide coverage for dog bites, broken windows, etc. Certainly you should have accident or medical insurance to cover injuries to your own kid.

Some people don't have to worry about expense, but are not willing to invest time and effort. The horse requires a lot of both.

Taking care of the horse is a daily and a year-around job. You can put a bicycle in the garage, skis on a rack, a dog or cat in a kennel, empty your swimming pool, and go off on a trip without worrying about what you left behind. Not so if you own a horse, even if he is kept in a boarding stable. In addition to feeding the horse, someone has to see that the horse is ridden or exercised regularly.

Keeping a horse at home instead of in a boarding stable is an even bigger responsibility. *The horse will be completely dependent upon your kid (with support from the family) for survival.* The first requisite is that your kid *knows how* to take care of the horse. The second requisite is that your kid *will spend the time* to take care of and exercise the horse. If the horse is standing around without proper care and exercise he will probably cost more in the long run when you count up the vet bills.

The horse must be fed at least two times each day, must be given adequate water, and should have his stall mucked out (cleaned out) at least once each day; twice is better.

In most cases, it is the parent's responsibility to call the farrier (horseshoer) and make an appointment with him. The farrier must be given enough notice so he can find time for your horse in his schedule, and you will have to be there when the farrier comes, even if it means waiting several hours. A horseshoer or farrier who knows his business well and is reliable (comes when he says he will) is one to be treasured. One of the oldest sayings in the horse world is, "No foot, no horse." You never save money by putting off getting the farrier or by getting an incompetent but less-expensive farrier to take care of a horse. Another benefit of boarding your kid's horse in a stable is being able to use their regular shoer. Stable personnel usually will arrange for the horse to be shod, and even hold the horse.

Unfortunately, there are a number of horse-owners who should never own horses. The SPCA receives many calls from people who see horses with inadequate feed and care. Whether the horse's poor condition is the result of ignorance or carelessness, he suffers just the same.

It is absolutely essential to provide the horse with his basic needs at all times. If your family cannot afford to take care of a horse properly without wondering about what it will do to your budget, or worry-

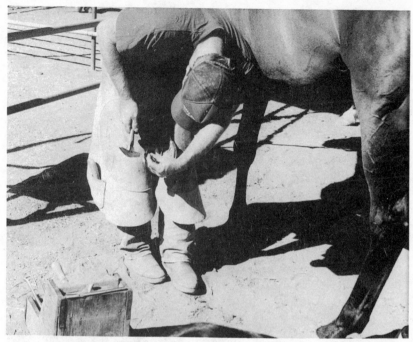

A horseshoer who not only shoes your kid's horse correctly but comes when he says he will is a treasure.

ing about who is going to end up taking care of him, please don't get a horse no matter how much your kid wants one. It is not fair to this generous and courageous animal who of necessity is completely at the mercy of his owner.

So if the answer is no, what are you going to tell your kid? As my Aunt Margo says, "You can't have everything; not all at once." If your kid is truly dedicated to horses, real horses and not just the dream stuff, she will find a way to be with them. She will be drawn to working with them, and eventually she will own one. But I'm not in favor of parents getting bent out of shape to buy a horse when their kid will be better off accomplishing that through her own efforts when she is older.

If you live in an area remote from stables and ranches and horses, give your kid some good non-fiction horse books and let her store up knowledge that she will some day use. If she can't have a horse right now, it isn't the end of the world. A kid is better off having something to work for than having it handed to her by someone else's sacrifice.

If you do live in a "horsey" area, you can encourage your kid to find horse owners who need help (what horse owner doesn't?) and start out on a volunteer basis. The owner has to know your kid is reliable, follows orders competently, and above all, takes seriously the responsibility of horse care. She can begin with mucking out stalls and cleaning tack and acting as Girl Friday for the horse owner. She can learn a lot about horses that some day will stand her in good stead. Many a great rider started out by mucking stalls in someone's stable.

It isn't the end of the world if your kid can't have a horse. The Pegasus B Team gives an inspiring demonstration of vaulting, or gymnastics on a moving horse.

An exciting alternative for horse ownership is getting involved in the sport of "vaulting." There might even be a vaulting team in your area. Vaulting is the art of gymnastics performed on a moving horse. A team consists of a horse, a trainer, and eight youngsters not over 16 years of age. The horse is controlled by the trainer who keeps the horse on a long line trotting or cantering in a circle around the trainer. The horse wears a special "vaulting rig," a leather harness that fastens around the horse. It has handles and straps on it for the kids to hold on to as they jump up, climb around doing gymnastics, and jump off the horse. As many as three youngsters can be on top of the horse at once, forming a pyramid and other daring figures.

Vaulting is a very popular sport because it is exhilarating for the participants and beautiful to watch. It teaches balance, coordination, muscular development, and teamwork, along with the thrill of working with a horse who clearly enjoys having the kids romping around on top.

The sport is well organized on an international level with competitions around the world. Like figure skating, it has compulsory figures to be performed, and then free style riding to show off special talents.

There are vaulting teams for tiny tots and even for adults. Vaulting is also an excellent means of enabling a kid to conquer the fear that occasionally comes after a bad fall while riding. It's good for adults under the same circumstances, too!

The address of the American Vaulting Association is listed in the Resource Guide.

If, after careful consideration, you still think that it's a good idea for your family to have a horse, you'll want to know what the horse's basic needs are. There are lots of books for dedicated horsepersons, but you're not a horseperson, yet. I'll try to give you a "crash course" for parents.

Chapter 11

The Bare Necessities: Food, Shelter, And Love

Basic horse care....feeding is art as well as science....
roughage, concentrates, salt, succulents, water....what
determines diet....rule of thumb....how digestion
works....10 rules of feeding....shelter....exercise
....companionship or love.

It may be hard to believe, but some kids can take riding lessons for years without being aware of what is essential for a horse's well-being. Sure, the kid might say, he needs hay and water and a place to live. Well, what kind of hay? How much water? What constitutes good living quarters? And what more does a horse need?

Most kids taking riding lessons have a great deal to learn before they can be entrusted with the ownership of a horse. It is the responsibility of the parent to see that the kid has a good foundation in horse care both from books and from experienced horsemen before the family considers horse ownership. It's like "driver's ed" in school before letting a kid get behind the wheel of a car.

To state it simply, horses need food and water, shelter, exercise, and—yes—companionship or love.

Horses in the wild were able to take care of themselves very well. Well enough for them to survive 50 million years. It was when man took over their management that they ran into trouble. The way we keep and feed horses is not normal for the horse, but we do it because it is convenient for us. Good stable management and good horse care try to duplicate nature as much as possible, and to make up for what the horse is no longer allowed to do for himself.

Feeding horses correctly is an art as well as a science. People can get along eating junk food, although it will affect their health in later years, but a horse has to have the right stuff for horses from the beginning or he won't grow up or stay healthy. Many books and articles have been written on the subject of equine nutrition, and some good ones are listed at the back of this book. Be sure that one or two are in your home for permanent reference if a horse is going to be part of your household.

Horses need three kinds of foods – those which build and repair the body, those which provide energy for the body, and those which aid digestion. All the nutrients a horse needs can be supplied by *roughage*, *concentrates*, *salt*, *succulents*, and *water*.

Roughage is the word applied to bulk foods such as the different kinds of pasture grass and hay.

Concentrates are defined as feeds with concentrated nutrition such as grains, grain mixtures, and hay mixed with grain and processed into pellets.

Succulents are any green or juicy food, such as grass, alfalfa or lucerne, carrots, apples, turnips, beets, parsnips, etc. Hay when green and growing is a succulent; when cut, dried, and baled it is roughage. Lawn clippings should not be fed as they frequently cause colic.

Water, and a lot of it, is essential. Every 24 hours the salivary glands of a horse produce about 10 gallons of saliva to aid digestion. To produce that much saliva, a horse must drink between 8 and 12 gallons of water daily.

The correct diet for a horse depends upon three things: his size, his individual temperament, and the kind of work he is asked to do. Size is obvious. A pony doesn't need as much food as a draft horse. Temperament refers to his disposition, such as easy-going or nervous. A horse who has no trouble keeping weight on is known as an "easy keeper." A horse who eats a lot without putting on weight is known as a "poor keeper." "Kind of work" means any kind of riding, from trail riding to steeplechasing, as well as growing, pregnancy, nursing a foal, and breeding.

The horse must be fed not only by formula, but "by eye." A horse should be in good flesh for the work he is asked to do. For the ordinary riding horse, you should be able to feel his ribs by pushing against his sides, but you should not be able to see them. Only race horses and endurance horses can be "ribby" when well fed because they are bone and muscle and have practically no stored fat.

A horse needs the same nutrients that humans do: carbohydrates, proteins, fats, vitamins, minerals, and water, but he needs them in different proportions than humans, and from very different sources.

Knowing what to feed a horse is not enough—knowing *how much* to feed him is just as important. The quantity of each of the types of feed should be determined by *weight* and not by volume. The bulk of his diet is in hay.

Hay comes in bales, very small ones on the East coast weighing 45-50 pounds and easy to lift, and big heavy ones on the West coast weighing an average of 125 pounds, although I have seen some as heavy as 145 pounds per bale. Bales are bound with special twine or wire. When the bale is cut open, it usually fans out in small flat bundles four to six inches thick called "flakes" or "leaves."

A single flake can weigh anywhere from four or five pounds in a loosely packed bale to ten or twelve pounds in a heavy bale. This is why you can't say a horse should be fed a certain number of flakes of hay unless you've weighed them and know how much hay he would be getting. Experienced stable help can tell about how much a flake weighs, but for the novice, a household scales in the barn is a worthwhile investment. You want to give the horse enough to eat but you don't want to waste feed.

Commercial stables usually feed hay that is native to the locality. There are three types of hay—grass hay such as timothy, grain hay such as oat or rye, and legume hay such as alfalfa or lucerne. In most parts of the country, timothy hay is the favored grass hay, and lucerne or alfalfa the favored legume hay. Good quality alfalfa can meet all of the nutritional needs of a horse who is worked less than five hours a week, but alfalfa is not readily available in all parts of the country.

Stables often feed one kind of hay in the morning and another in the evening for economy and to give the horse variety. In the west, oat hay and alfalfa are a frequent combination. When storage is a problem, hay coarsely cut and compressed into cubes can be used. Hay cubes are more expensive than long hay, but take about one-third the storage space.

The most common grains are oats, barley, and corn. They are not given whole, but rolled or crushed or crimped to make digestion easier. Grains are necessary for energy. A horse that's being ridden or worked needs to have grain added to his diet on his work days. Oats are often the preferred grain, since more can be given with less risk of over-feeding. In feed stores you will find ready-mixes containing several kinds of grains mixed with molasses, called sweet feed. Pelleted feed is alfalfa chopped and mixed with grain, steamed, compressed, and cut into pellets.

The biggest advantage of pellets is their taking less storage space than hay. When storage is at a premium, this is important, but sometimes a cheaper grade of alfalfa is used because it cannot be identified in the pellet. Recently "extruded" feeds have come on the market—alfalfa chopped with added grain and then "popped" like puffed wheat instead of steamed and compressed. It is more expensive than pellets but less likely to cause colic because it is lighter and horses take longer to eat it.

Another important concentrate is wheat bran, from the feed store, not the grocery. Served dampened as a bran mash (see Ch. 20) or dry and given once or twice a week, it aids digestion and adds bulk.

Salt is absolutely essential. It is offered to horses usually in a salt block put in a bucket or manger in his stall. Plain salt comes in a white block; salt with trace minerals comes in a red block. The trace mineral salt block furnishes all the necessary minerals. Loose salt can be given at each meal, but some horses won't eat it. Most prefer having a salt block they can lick from time to time.

A little bit of knowledge is a dangerous thing, but I'll risk giving you a rule of thumb for quantity of feed— approximately 2 to 3 pounds of feed for each 100 pounds that a horse weighs. A horse that weighs around 1000 pounds might eat about 20 pounds of feed per day. Pregnant and/or nursing mares, like human mothers, need more nutritious diets. So do young foals and growing horses, just like children. In Chapter 20 I'll tell you how to figure the weight of a horse without scales.

I suggest your kid study what the experts have written about feeding horses. Encourage your kid to learn how to calculate a horse's diet. It is not easy, but it is vital to the horse's well-being. Both the 4-H and U.S. Pony Clubs teach equine nutrition.

Knowing *how* a horse eats is almost as important as knowing what and how much he eats. The horse's digestive system is unique.

A horse's anatomy is hooked up differently from man's. Man can breathe through his mouth; horses cannot. Man can cough up something objectionable; horses can do it only with great difficulty. Man can vomit; horses rarely can, and the vomitus exits through the nose and never through the mouth. Thus it is imperative that the horse's feed be of the best quality. Any feed that is moldy or spoiled can have fatal consequences.

The horse is designed to eat by grazing, to have some food in his system always, but never very much at one time so he can be ready to run. Since nature wants him to eat little and often, his stomach is very small compared to his size. Because the stomach is so small, almost all of the digestion is carried on in the large intestine. And that large intestine is unusual.

Most of the digestion of food is actually carried out not by digestive juices, but *by friendly bacteria present in the cecum and great colon*. It is because of the friendly bacteria that horses can eat hay while man can not. These bacteria perform many valuable functions. An important one is transforming the fibrous part of roughage into volatile fatty acids which produce energy for the horse. The bacteria are dependent upon what the horse eats, and quickly die without sufficient and systematic nourishment. When the life-cycle of the bacteria is disturbed, the horse suffers a severe intestinal ailment called colic.

With this general idea of the way a horse's digestive system works, you can understand why the following ten principles of good feeding have been established:

1. A horse should be fed smaller amounts and several times a day rather than a large amount once a day.

2. A horse should be allowed adequate grazing, or be fed enough hay so that his digestive system always has roughage in it. Oat hay or straw in front of the horse at all times gives him something to pick at and cuts down on stable vices developed from boredom.

3. A horse should be fed according to his size, his temperament, and the work he is asked to do. In general, when he is working hard, he should be given more of the concentrated foods such as grain. When he is idle, he should have his grain cut back or omitted.

4. A horse should be fed at the same times each day so that the friendly bacteria can work on their own schedule and not die out.

5. Any change in the diet or feeding routine should be very gradual and spread over a number of days so the friendly bacteria can adjust to the change.

6. A horse should be given only the best quality feed as he may become ill with feed that is questionable.

7. A horse should not be worked hard when his stomach is full right after a big feed. The stomach is next to the chest and his breathing can be affected adversely.

8. A horse should have a salt block always available, preferably one that has trace minerals, so he can take salt as he needs it. A few horses will gobble down their salt block. These horses should be given a daily ration of loose salt (available with trace minerals from the feed dealer).

9. A horse should have plenty of water available. An active horse will drink from 8 to 12 gallons of water a day.

10. If water is not constantly available, a horse must be offered water before being fed.

When these rules of good feeding are followed, horses seldom come down with that most common and serious of equine ailments — colic.

Besides food and water, a horse needs some kind of shelter. In the wild, horses found shelter with each other among trees, in ravines, and other natural places. They have to have shelter from moisture and from wind.

Once in a while a horse will enjoy standing in a light summer rain, and sometimes in falling snow when it's coming straight down in big lazy flakes, but he usually prefers shelter. He also needs shelter from a blazing summer sun to prevent sun stroke, and he *must* have shelter from wind.

A horse has his own system of insulation in his coat, and he changes his coat twice a year. In the spring, he sheds his winter coat and grows a thin glossy coat of hair for summer. In the fall, he sheds his summer coat, and grows a winter coat that has two kinds of hair. One is short, dense fine hair, and the other is long, rough, coarse hair. Between these two kinds of hair is trapped a blanket of air which provides excellent insulation against the cold. When wind hits the horse, it separates the coarse outer hair, letting the air blanket escape so that the horse becomes chilled. Protection against wind is of prime importance. Oils and dander in the winter coat make it nearly waterproof.

Stalls and three-sided sheds can provide adequate protection from wind. Boarding stables usually have stalls to provide shelter. If a horse is kept in a paddock or pasture, a simple shed open on one side with its back wall to the prevailing winds will give the horse the protection he needs. If the barn or shed has a large overhang, it will also provide shade.

Another requirement for a horse is exercise. Nature designed the horse to roam over vast distances. His survival depended upon his running mechanism. When man "tamed" the horse, he kept the horse in small areas for his own convenience, eventually shutting him up in little rooms which he called stalls. Imagine what it would be like to be shut in a small room all day and all night with only an hour or two outside. It is little wonder that some horses develop stable vices like weaving (standing and swaying back and forth), biting, kicking, and chewing on fences, from sheer boredom. They don't have enough to do.

If a horse is kept in a stall or other small area, he must be taken out for exercise at least an hour a day, and if possible be given a chance to exercise himself turned out in a paddock or pasture. In some areas boarding stables have stalls with adjoining paddocks or "runs" so the horses can go in and out at will. The two brightest spots in a horse's daily life are meal time and exercise time. Your kid will certainly have time during the summer to ride and give the horse the exercise he must have, but what about during the school year? The horse's needs come first. Does she realize this?

There is one last requirement for a horse's well-being. You may not think it is a necessity, but it surely is. Like humans, horses need companionship or love.

Shari is "family" to her POA whom she calls Brat. He's a happy pony with her companionship.

The horse is a herd animal because of his instinct for survival. The many eyes, ears, and nostrils of the herd could sense danger more quickly than the senses of a single animal. There was security in belonging to a herd.

Taking the horse away from his herd and his natural habitat doesn't eliminate his inner need for companionship. When a horse is kept in a barn or in a paddock, it's best for him to at least be able to see and talk to other horses.

A horse needs friendship, someone to love and be loved by. It is important that his owner understand this. The horse must either have the company of other animals or receive love and attention from his owner. If the horse is stabled alone without much attention, he can survive, but he will not be a happy horse.

Earlier we discussed how horses develop friendships with animals of different species. This ability of the horse to form a satisfying relationship with a different species is the basis for the strong bond that can develop between a horse and rider. This bond makes possible acts of courage and love that neither could perform with a different partner. Such combinations are famous in military history and equine sports, but also exist among many backyard horses and their riders. Ask any long-time horseman about his favorite horse at a certain time in his life, and watch his face light up.

If your kid has convinced you that she is willing to undertake the responsibility for the care of the horse, will feed him and exercise him and love him, with your help and financial support as a parent, then you can give serious consideration to buying a horse.

Chapter 12

Preparing For The Plunge

*Get ready before purchase....boarding stable....
someone's backyard....your backyard....zoning....
location....portable vs. frame....ventilation....
storage....fencing....gates....latches....manure
disposal....feed supply.*

Buying a horse is more like acquiring a new member of the family than it is like buying a car or a major appliance.

When you knew you were going to have a baby, you began shopping for the new arrival—a crib or bassinet, a layette, nursing bottles, toys, a baby carrier, and you may even have re-painted and decorated one room to be a nursery. You had everything ready for the baby in advance.

Preparing for a horse is quite a project, too, and all the preparations should be made *before you buy the horse.*

If your kid is taking lessons, you will probably want to keep her horse at the stable where her instructor is. Or if the instructor travels to different boarding stables, you might even have a choice of stables, and the instructor will be a help in deciding.

You will need to make reservations in advance for the stall or paddock. If you do have a choice, check out the facilities of the stables before you decide. Ideally, a stable will furnish good shelter, good feed, fresh water, access to a riding ring and/or trails, a place for the horse to exercise on the days when your kid can't ride him, and a place for your kid's tack. It should be clean and orderly.

Look at the horses kept in that stables to see the care that is given at the barn. If the horses look well-fed, happy, and clean, your kid's horse probably will be too.

Stables when well-built have lofty high ceilings, good drainage, good ventilation, and no drafts. Windows (protected by heavy mesh) are hinged at the bottom and open inward at the top so that fresh air is available without causing a draft. When you walk into a properly ventilated, well-built barn, the air inside will never be stale air.

A barn tightly closed against outside air quickly becomes stuffy. This noxious air fosters respiratory ailments and eye inflammations. It also lowers a horse's resistance to disease. Stalls with partitions that rise only five or so feet high with wire mesh from the partition to the roof are preferable to fully enclosed stalls.

In cold climates, barns may be well-insulated and heated and have fans to ensure good ventilation and fresh air. In mild climates the barns may be largely open. Where it is mild, open air paddocks with three-sided shelters can be more desirable than stalls. Such shelters afford protection against wind, have natural temperature, good air circulation, and room for the horse to move about.

The sides of the stall or shelter must be smooth and free from potential dangers such as hooks, bolts, nails and splinters which might injure a horse. A clay floor is the best flooring, and some kind of bedding— shavings, straw, or sawdust—must be provided, so the horse can lie down in comfort when he wishes. Check on the bedding to see that there is plenty of it in the stalls, and that each stall is cleaned at least once a day and preferably twice.

Most important is the feed supply. Look at the kind of hay in the mangers, and at the hay storage. Even if you've never before seen hay up close, you should be able to tell something about its quality. The hay should be sweet-smelling and not dusty. The hay in storage for the stable should be afforded adequate protection from moisture, both from the ground and from the sky.

The water buckets or self-waterers and feed tubs should be clean also. The water buckets should never be empty, and the water should be fresh. Horses are picky about water. Sometimes horses will drop from dehydration before they drink foul water.

The ideal stable has a paddock or "run" opening from each stall so the horse can go in and out and exercise himself at will. Pastures for half-day turn-outs are popular in many places. There should be a good-sized arena for riding, and hopefully even access to trails.

A tack room or place for your kid's tack is usually included in the board bill. It should be large enough also for barrels of grain, buckets, rakes, and similar paraphernalia. When you walk into the tack room of a stable, it should smell good—of oiled leather.

The services that each stable offers for horses vary enormously. *Be sure to have in writing exactly what services are included in the board bill, and the cost of services available but which are not included.* Services are the feeding of grain and any supplements in addition to the basic hay, the kind and amount of stall bedding, mucking out of stall or paddock, putting on and taking off horse blankets daily, turning the horse out for exercise, holding the horse for veterinarian or shoer, giving medication, etc. Some barns have a high basic board bill which includes many services. Other barns start with a low board bill, but by the time they have added on all the services, the total can be astronomical. If the stable is run in a business-like way, they probably will have a contract for you to sign which spells out exactly who is responsible for what and when. Read it carefully before you sign.

You might have to go on a waiting list for the stable of your choice, and board the horse somewhere else till your kid's name comes up. Even though your kid is on the waiting list, it pays to phone the stable manager every week or so to remind him that you have not made other arrangements.

If you are going to keep your horse in someone else's backyard, it should certainly be the yard of a knowledgeable horse person. To have the horse watched over by someone who knows nothing about horses will surely lead to disaster. Horses are not suicidal, but sometimes they seem that way. Their problems occur because their instincts are based on an entirely different environment from the man-made one in which we force them to live.

Backyard facilities should afford the same basics as a boarding stable only on a more informal scale—adequate shelter, good feed, fresh water, a place to exercise the horse or provide access to a riding ring, and a tack room. If having your kid feed the horse herself and muck out the stall is part of the financial arrangement, she must be able to go back and forth easily without involving another member of the family. Again, put down in writing exactly what the board bill includes, and which services are offered for what cost. This will help prevent unpleasant surprises later.

If the backyard horse is going to be turned out with other horses, someone is going to have to watch them for the first couple of weeks until the pecking order is established, and it becomes clear that all the horses are getting enough to eat.

You certainly don't want to see horses turned out in a field that is also used for disposing of junk. The presence of old car bodies, obsolete household appliances, broken fences, gates tied with rope, and mud holes for the horses to stand in, are probably indications of the way the horses will be looked after.

Since you are not a knowledgeable horse-person, you may wonder at the wisdom of keeping your kid's horse in your own backyard. There are pros and cons to that arrangement.

Keeping the horse at home means a lot more work, but there are also more rewards. Having your kid care for her horse by herself is a big responsibility but it can build good character and help her mature. The bond between the kid and the horse will be established more quickly. You will enjoy being able to watch them. Best of all, your family will be better able to appreciate what your kid is undertaking.

It also means that from time to time you may have to help her with the horse. Maybe not a lot, but there's the possibility, more than just holding the reins while she dashes off for a pit stop. As a parent I'm sure you've learned that you do what you have to do, even though you may not like it.

If you are absolutely adamant about not helping with the horse, your household will be happier if the horse is not kept at your house. Even if you are sure that your kid knows your feelings, respects them, and has made other arrangements for help when she needs it, there's bound to come a time when she'll need a parent, and desperately. If you've read this far, I doubt if you would turn her down.

If you are sure that your kid's horse will be kept at someone else's stable or back yard, you can skip the rest of this chapter and go directly to the next one, Chapter 13. But regardless of where the horse will be kept, it's time for you to start reading some of those books meant for the owner of a horse. Although the horse may be your kid's, indirectly his well-being is in your hands as well.

If you still think you might like to have that horse in your own backyard, read on.

The first thing to do is check out your local zoning laws. If your property was formerly horse property when you bought it, possibly with a horse shelter and good fencing, your preparations will be minimal. Otherwise, you have some work ahead of you. Make sure the facilities are covered by the *present* zoning laws.

The horse will need the same basics he would at the boarding stable. In addition you will have to make provision for storage of hay, grain, and other feed, for bales of shavings or straw for bedding, and a place for all the buckets, rakes, wheelbarrows, tools, and other things that horsekeeping attracts.

If your backyard or land has no horse improvements on it and you are starting from scratch, remember that the design for a horse barn is quite different from the design for a garage or a tool shed. Consult an expert on horse barns if you can, and start reading the books recommended for horse housing.

You may not have much choice of location. It may be decided by the location of neighboring buildings, especially if you have a suburban lot or small pasture. Find out from the Planning Department how far away from property lines and other buildings the horse shelter must be built.

You are fortunate if you have larger acreage and varied terrain and a choice of where to build. The location is important. The barn or shelter should not be built on top of a hill because of wind, nor in a low spot because of lack of drainage. If level ground is not available, the side of a slope making a small cut and minimum fill is the best choice. You need to take into account the prevailing winds and the possibility of flies and odors with relation to neighbors as well as to your own family.

A well-constructed small barn utilizing a hillside, with a cupola for ventilation.

There are two types of buildings to choose from for the horse's shelter—pre-fabricated and frame.

The pre-fabricated or "portable stall" or barn is the simplest way to go. It can be quickly installed on a prepared leveled dirt pad. The advantage is its ease of installation and, because it is portable, you may not need a building permit. If later you should move to another home, you could dismantle the barn and take it with you. A great many companies manufacture pre-fabricated stalls and barns, and you will be flooded with material when you start writing for brochures.

Study the pre-fabricated barn construction carefully. Some are beautiful but do not have provision for good ventilation. The biggest problem stables have is build-up of moisture from animal heat. Under a low metal roof the stalls may get hot and stuffy. Good ventilation can be ensured by spaces under the eaves, louvres, or a cupola or wind turbine on the roof.

The importance of ventilation was noted more than a hundred years ago by Dr. Griffith Evans of Wales, who is now called the Father of Veterinary Medicine. He was in charge of moving troops and 106 horses on a six days' overland march to Liverpool, England. He observed that some horses on the march each day perspired sooner and much more than the others—and invariably they were the ones that had been stabled in closed, badly-ventilated quarters the night before. The ones kept overnight in well-ventilated stables had no problems on the next day's march.

If you are going to build from scratch, it's wise to hire a licensed contractor who is aware of the requirements of horse shelter, or acquire plans from a company that specializes in this construction. Some places which have plans for barns are listed in the Recommended Reading.

The simplest shelter is the three-sided shed. The walls must be at least 2" thick and 8' high. The roof should slant and, if you're in a rainy climate, have rain gutters to prevent run-off ditches. A minimum space of about 12' x 12' should be allowed for each horse. The roof could have an overhang for additional shade.

Either in the hay storage place or tack room there should be room for covered rodent-proof cans for grain and feed supplements, and for first aid supplies for horses. The construction should be such that there is no possibility of the horse's gaining access to the feed, or your kid will have a very sick horse some day. You'll also need a room adjoining

A portable barn where this Paint Horse can live comfortably. Notice the ventilation slots just above the stall walls.

or near the stall as a place for your kid's tack so it doesn't all end up in her bedroom. There should be a saddle rack, a bridle rack, a shelf for grooming kit, etc.

If hay bales in your area are heavy, you'll need hay hooks for moving the bales. You will also need wire cutters near the hay storage for cutting open the bales of hay. Wire cutters disappear quickly unless you drill a hole in a piece of board about 12" long, paint it a bright color, and then attach it to the cutters with several feet of rope.

For the horse to have proper exercise, some kind of well-fenced paddock or corral or pasture must be available. The type of fencing is very important. The cost of the different types will depend upon which part of the country you're in, and what is available. Fencing materials can be of steel or iron pipe, post and board rails, post and pole rails, electric fencing, and wire fencing. The new plastic-coated fences are beautiful and strong with practically no maintenance, although their initial cost is high.

The smaller the area to be fenced, the stronger and more rigid the fencing must be.

For small paddocks or corrals, metal fencing can be used. Galvanized pipe, 1-7/8" outside diameter preferred, is available in sections for corrals. The sections are from three to five rails high, and come in lengths from 6' to 24'. A small paddock should be at least 5' high. The lowest rail should be several feet above the ground so a horse lying down near the fence cannot get his legs caught underneath. Gate sections are available also. The sections are easily assembled and bolted together. Maintenance is minimal, but cost usually makes pipe fencing impractical for large areas.

Board fencing is less expensive than metal fencing for large areas, and can make a good-looking fence. It should be four feet high. The wooden posts must be at least 6" in diameter and sunk 30" in the ground, the posts treated with a good preservative. Railroad ties make excellent fence posts. Posts should be set not more than 8' apart. The boards should be at least 2" thick and 6" or 8" wide with a minimum of 3 rails.

Rough-cut lumber, sometimes called corral lumber, is very reasonable in some parts of the country. It is about 2" x 6" and comes in 16' lengths, ideal for setting on posts that are 8' apart. The joining of the boards must alternate on the posts to increase the strength. That is, the first and third rails could have joints on the same post, but the second and fourth rails would have their joints on the posts before and after it. Rails are always set on the inside of the posts so they can't be pushed loose by horses at play.

Unfortunately horses do chew wood, and boards do break when horses play around. The cost of maintenance is high, since the fence must be painted or sprayed with a waterproof stain or a preservative.

There are several paint products on the market which are supposed to be unappetizing to horses—but some horses, like some people, will eat anything. A temporary measure which I have found very effective is making a paste of cayenne pepper and water or salad oil and painting the top of each rail or board with the paste, using a small paint brush or basting brush.

A fairly secure fencing for horses in a large area is V-mesh wire, and in some cases woven wire or welded wire, with wooden posts. Never use steel fence T-posts. They not only bend but can be driven through a horse's chest or neck while he is playing around. The disadvantage of wire is that the horse can catch the end of his shoe in it if he should kick or paw near the fence. The openings of the wire fence must be so small that a horse can not possibly get his foot through if he kicks near the fence. Sheep wire can catch a whole foot in the squares and cut up the horse. Barbed wire is completly undesirable for horses, especially in a small area of a few acres. Even when hundreds of acres are fenced with barbed wire, sooner or later horses will get hurt on it.

Electric fencing is suitable for a temporary enclosure, or for existing fences that horses are prone to chew. Aluminum wire, #12 or #15 gauge, will break more readily than steel wire—and breaking may prevent a horse getting cut up if he does run into the fence. The ideal height is about 3' high. The insulators should be put on the outside of the posts to prevent injury to a playful horse. The posts can be set from

The Kiwi Gate Latch® made by the Colorado Kiwi Company is easy for a child to open and close, even with mittens or gloves on. Although this latch baffles our cleverest horse, Kalani, the manufacturer suggests a simple wire be run through the catch link for the first week if you have a real Houdini horse.

Lawrence Brothers came up with this neat design for a gate latch. Only a little harder to open than the Kiwi, none of our horses have figured this one out.

12' to 15' apart. A horse cannot see a single wire strand from a distance. Flagging the fence with short pieces of bright surveyor tape can serve as a reminder to the horse where the wire is.

The building of proper gates is an art in itself. Horse gates should be a minimum of 4' wide and hung on absolutely solid posts. Ideally, they can be opened and shut with one hand, leaving the other completely free to hang on to a horse that may be jumping around. Their framework must be rigid, and the latches must be as horse-proof as possible, especially in the fencing of small areas.

Snap-locks are not horse-proof. Most horses can open them easily with their lips. There are at least two latches on the market that can be operated with one hand, yet are extremely difficult for even a Houdini horse to open. The latch must be easy for a kid to open and close with one hand, even with mittens on if you live in a cold climate.

The better the stable and fencing arrangements, the less frequent the accidents to a horse. For more detailed information about buildings, fences, and gates, see the Recommended Reading.

To be entirely practical, arrangements must be made for manure disposal. A 1000 pound horse produces between 30 and 40 pounds of manure in one day, of which 20% is moisture. Your kid may get more exercise than she bargained for when she starts cleaning the stall or paddock at least once a day. Twice is better. She will need a pitchfork if the stall bedding is straw, and a manure rake for bare ground and for bedding of sawdust or shavings. After picking up the manure, she can dump it into a wheelbarrow to take to the disposal place. A large lightweight wheelbarrow with a rubber tire makes a difficult job a lot easier.

In some towns and suburban areas, trash collection companies have an arrangement to pick up trash cans of manure on certain days of the week for an additional fee. You'll need several substantial trash cans for the manure—it is quite heavy until spread out and dried.

Where commercial disposal is not available, until the manure can be hauled away permanently, a manure pit is the most useful arrangement for disposal. The "pit" consists of an area enclosed by a low cement block wall (or similar material) into which the manure can be thrown after removal from the stall. The manure should be turned over with a pitchfork from time to time and kept covered with a thick plastic tarpaulin. This helps prevent odors and the spread of disease. In two weeks, any fly eggs present are killed by the heat so generated. Manure treated in this way can be spread in riding arenas and on bridle paths.

In rural areas, horse manure is very useful as a fertilizer, but fresh manure must never be spread on pastures where horses will graze. It's fine to spread it on fields that will be ploughed, or disked at least 3" deep, and then planted. The beneficial effects as fertilizer are cumulative.

About half of the nutrients in the manure are utilized by plants in the first year, half of the remainder in the second year, and so on. The organic matter is also a valuable addition to the soil.

In some parts of the country, manure from soiled straw bedding is in demand by mushroom and vegetable growers. You might be able to work out a satisfactory arrangement with them.

You can buy stable and grooming tools but no halter, saddle, bridle, or saddle pads until you have purchased the horse and know his size and shape.

Last, but equally important, you will need to be assured of a steady source of good feed. Check with other horse people to learn of their suppliers and how satisfied they are with them. You will want to buy a ton of hay at a time if you have a safe place to store that much. By the ton is cheaper than by the bale and delivery charges add up.

Since it may take quite a while to find the right horse, you don't want to lay in a supply of feed—yet. Just be ready to have it delivered when you need it.

Once you have completed all these preparations so your kid's horse will feel at home after being unloaded from the trailer, you are ready to begin the search for the horse.

Chapter 13

Make A List And Check It Twice

Falling for first horse.... list essential qualities: disposition, ground manners, sensible age, reasonable size, sufficient training, good conformation, serviceably sound, negative Coggins.... non-essential list.

A well-known and highly respected horseshoer once gave a talk before our local horse club. He announced that he would talk about horses' hooves and shoeing, after which he would answer questions from the audience. "But first," he said, "I want to ask all of you one question." He paused to be sure he had everyone's attention. In a tone of great exasperation he said, "Why in *!*#** do some of you buy the horses that you buy?"

A roar of laughter filled the room, for every one of us knew of cases where horses were bought that should never have been bought, and then the shoer was asked to "fix up the horse's feet."

When the farrier could make himself heard again, he said, "I'll answer that myself. It's because your ten-year-old daughter was standing beside you, looking at that horse with tears in her eyes, saying, 'Oh, Daddy, he's the most beautiful horse in the world and he's the one I want.' That horse may be pigeon-toed, calf-kneed, cow-hocked, and have splints and bowed tendons, but when your daughter bats her eyelashes at you and says, 'Oh, Daddy, did you see how he *looked* at me?' it would take somebody with a heart of stone to say no."

More laughter. But oh what a world of truth in his words!

Yes, you should take your daughter with you when you look for a horse, but don't begin shopping until you both have a firm idea of what you need to look for. Once they know they're actually shopping for a horse, kids ten to twelve years old have a tendency to fall madly in love with the very first horse they look at. This happens so frequently I wouldn't ignore the possibility.

Perhaps the kid's wanting to buy the very first horse, no matter what, may arise from a subconscious fear that if the parent doesn't buy this particular horse, the parent will change his mind and not buy any at all. You might make a bargain with your kid—that the two of you will look at a minimum of four or five horses before any decision is made. If your kid knows she will be looking at that many, she may be able to keep from losing her heart to the first one.

For the next step in your search, I suggest you make a list of the qualities essential for your kid's horse. If you ask your kid to make a

Ileene is only five, but her pinto pony, Joker, is right for her because of his size and disposition.

list it would probably consist of one requirement—a chestnut mare with four white socks and a blazed face. She needs help!

First, disposition is more important than looks and breeding. The horse should have a good attitude and temperament and not be upset easily. He should be calm, steady, and dependable, without the tendency to shy at things.

Good ground manners are very important, and Cynthia, 14, is happy because her half-Welsh pony, Bronwen, is always easy to bridle.

If your kid is the high-strung type, she would be more comfortable with a quiet and easy-going horse. A quiet rider sometimes can steady a very sensitive horse as long as he doesn't upset her. A bold and energetic rider might enjoy riding a bold horse. No matter what your kid's personality, you must avoid a horse that is "too much horse," that is, more difficult than your kid can handle. Nothing turns off a rider's enthusiasm quicker than being afraid of her own horse. Neither do you want a "clunker," a horse that needs to be kicked soundly before moving. That type of horse discourages good riding posture and habits.

Second, the horse should have good ground manners. This means easy to catch and lead, to groom and work around, with no vices like biting, kicking, pulling back on his halter, not liking to have his feet picked out, being hard to bridle, etc. The kid should be able to catch the horse and get him ready by herself, with little or no help from a grown-up.

Third, a sensible age. The younger the kid, the better to have an older horse. By the time a horse is six, he is considered to be grown up and has begun to have some sense. He is less likely to want to goof off with other horses, or act like a kid and play funny tricks with his rider out on the trail. His price tag is at its highest in this age bracket because he has many years ahead of him.

By the time he is twelve he should have a lot of experience and be able to take good care of his rider. The pricetag goes down after twelve years or so, supposedly because the horse doesn't have many years left. A horse even older than that is sometimes a good investment. With good feeding and good care, even a fifteen-year-old will still have some valuable years left to give to a young rider. I have known wonderful horses in their twenties that you would never guess were over fifteen. For sheer baby-sitting ability, there's nothing like an elderly mare with strong maternal instincts.

Unless the horse is registered with papers, you cannot be certain of the horse's exact age, no matter what the seller says, because the horse will never tell you his birthday. In some cases it is possible to get a fairly good idea of his age by his teeth. We'll deal with this subject later when we are looking at horses.

Fourth, a reasonable size, depending on the size of your kid. It's good to have a horse that the kid can handle comfortably, but you don't want to put her on a horse which is too small for her. Her feet shouldn't be hanging way down below the horse's barrel (body). On the other hand, if your kid is short, she might always need help in bridling and saddling a tall horse. This is important if you want your kid to be independent instead of having someone there every time she gets ready to ride.

A favorite cartoon of mine shows a small child on a very tall horse. The child is so small the soles of her boots don't even come down to the bottom of the saddle. The child is complaining, "He won't listen to my legs." Why should he? He can't feel them.

Although large horses usually have a longer and more comfortable stride than small horses, it isn't always true. A large pony called Charlie was loaned to our children's horsemanship camp for use as a school horse. The pony was tried out by one of the staff, who immediately re-named the pony. "He strides like a great big horse!" the young man exclaimed. "He's not Charlie, he's gotta be Chuck." So Chuck it was!

Although Jacob is only four years old, he can lead his Morgan mare, Connie, and help groom her because she has a kind and gentle disposition.

Everyone, even the tallest kids, wanted to ride that pony; he was great.

Fifth, sufficient training with correct aids so your kid will be able to handle him and have him teach her what she needs to know. He should be easy to mount and ride, willing to leave the barn even without a companion, and be reliable on the trail.

How he got his training is important. When an owner says proudly, "I trained him myself," it pays to be skeptical, especially if the owner is a youngster. The "trainer" cannot teach the horse what he himself doesn't know. He may have omitted vital training, or he may have unwittingly taught the horse wrong. I have met a number of "trainers" of their own horses who did not know that every horse should have two leads at the canter, a left lead and a right lead. A horse trained to have only one lead is a handicap too big for a novice rider to cope with. It is extremely difficult to re-train a horse—he has a memory like a stone tablet. A horse which has had some training by an expert is much safer as a rule.

As for an untrained horse just broke to saddle, called "green broke," an old proverb says, "A green rider on a green horse is a bad color combination." Unless your kid is very talented and brave, and has an exceptionally capable instructor who is willing to undertake this monumental task, forget about having your novice kid train a green horse, no matter what other good qualities the horse has.

If your kid is enjoying learning how to jump and has a good jumping instructor, you will want a horse that is an honest jumper who has been schooled to take 3'6" fences nicely, even if your kid would not be jumping that high for quite a while.

Sixth, fairly good conformation. Conformation is the way the horse is built. No horse is perfect; you and your kid will have to decide which defects your kid is going to have to live with. You should be interested in conformation primarily as it will affect the horse's soundness, that is, the horse's not going lame because of the way he is built. For example, a very large Quarter Horse with little bitty feet will probably develop a lameness from calcium deposits known as ringbone because as he grows older his feet can't adequately support his weight. We'll discuss conformation further when you'll have a real horse in front of you.

Ten-year-old Bill rides a Connemara pony, Patrice, who is just the right size for him.

Seventh, be serviceably sound. This means sound enough for the purpose for which your kid intends to use him. Only a veterinarian can tell you this after a careful examination of the horse, called a "prepurchase vet check." Since vet checks cost money, you should request one only when you are seriously interested in a certain horse. In older horses, arthritis is the number one enemy, but it doesn't necessarily rule out purchase of the horse. It can be mild enough that the horse is stiff when first taken out, but he "warms out of it" after he has walked around a bit—just like some people. But there's a big difference between being stiff at the beginning of exercise, and being permanently lame from an injury. In some cases, especially in a more expensive horse, the vet may recommend taking x-rays of the horse's feet or legs.

In any case, having a pre-purchase vet check can save you much grief, even for an inexpensive horse. After all the time and effort you'll spend on finding a horse and having your kid fall in love with him, you don't want to discover two weeks later that the horse isn't sound, or he is blind in one eye, or that something will always be going wrong with him. Chapter 17 tells you how to go about getting a pre-purchase vet check.

Eighth, a negative Coggins test taken within three weeks of buying the horse if the state in which you live requires it. The disease called equine infectious anemia or EIA is deadly, infectious, and as of this writing, has no preventive vaccine. In many states, horses cannot enter that state or be entered in horse shows without a certificate of a negative Coggins test. The Coggins test can determine whether or not the horse has the disease. In some states, California for example, if the horse is a native of that state and you are certain you will not be transporting your kid's horse out of state, the horse might not need to have a negative Coggins certificate. Your vet will know the regulations of your state and recommendations for your area. Many persons believe that a Coggins test should always be required as a good insurance policy since the disease is almost always fatal, and the few who recover from it become carriers and are permanently quarantined.

A horse who has all of the good qualities listed above as essential will actually be hard to find, especially at a reasonable price. We have described a paragon of a horse, but it gives you something to aim for. Horse-hunting usually results in the buyer having to decide which qualities are the most important, and which he can sacrifice if he has to.

You can make a second list of non-essential qualities that would be nice to have as long as they are within your budget. These are things like having shots up to date, trailers well, lunges, is an easy keeper, and even a good mover. This is a term which an experienced horseman can explain to you when you are looking at horses. Later we'll discuss color, markings, breed, and other non-essentials.

Now that you have a better idea of what to look for, where do you start looking? You'll get some help in the next chapter.

Chapter 14

Some Perils of Purchase

*You need expert help. . . . instructor, friend, professional
. . . . do-it-yourself. . . . finding horses for sale. . . . selling
methods. . . . what to ask on phone. . . . the hackamore
and the tie-down.*

A person *with* extensive knowledge of horses doesn't have an easy time buying a horse. It can be an enormous problem for a person *without* experience. Yet your kid's well-being depends upon your choice. This is a good reason for you to get help from an expert if at all possible.

If your kid has been taking lessons from an experienced and reliable instructor, the instructor is the best place to start. He should know better than anyone else what kind of a horse would be good for your kid, and he will certainly have your kid's interests at heart. He will want her to be happy with her new horse so she will continue to ride and take lessons from him.

Tell the instructor how much you can afford so you can stay within your budget. If his stable is show-oriented and you are planning to buy a horse that your kid can enter in horse shows or similar competitions, the instructor might even know of some suitable horses that are for sale. He is in a good position to watch for that kind of horse when he is at other stables and shows.

It is possible that the instructor may be too busy to go horse-shopping with you—it is a time-consuming activity—but he might be able to suggest a person qualified to help you. Professionals are always paid for their time and expertise, by fee or on a commission basis. If you have more time than money, you could do some of the legwork yourself and then pay the professional a flat fee to check out the one or two horses you are seriously interested in.

Ideally, you might have a personal friend who is a knowledgeable horseman and who would help you without pay.

If your kid doesn't have a good instructor to help you go horse-hunting, your next best bet as a non-horse person is to find a reputable professional horseman to do the looking for you. Professional trainers make their living in part by buying and selling horses for clients. Their goal is finding the right horse for a client, not just selling him a horse, and their business grows in direct proportion to the number of satisfied clients.

The professionals who do this get ten or fifteen percent above the purchase price as a commission. The question you may ask yourself is not necessarily "Can I afford to pay the fee to have him look for a suitable horse for my kid?" Perhaps it should be, "Can I afford not to pay him the fee to find a suitable horse?" If you have in mind an above-average price to pay for a horse and you are not a horseman yourself, a good professional is worth the investment. There are few things more risky or full of disenchantment than horse-buying. Be sure the professional knows you are a serious buyer and not a window-shopper.

Maybe where you live it's impossible to find a reliable professional to help you, or financially it is out of the question. Don't despair—if you are patient and careful, you can still come up with a good horse for your kid.

Finding the right horse may take several months, or even longer if you're looking for something special and you don't mind having your kid jumping up and down putting on the pressure. But horses are constantly being bought and sold. There may not be a suitable horse on the market this week, or the next, but sooner or later several will show up. Eventually (usually when you've about given up) you'll find the horse that makes it all worthwhile.

Where do you find horses for sale? The first places to look are local reputable boarding and training stables. Ask the barn manager and the instructors, and look at the bulletin boards at the barns. Check out the bulletin boards in feed stores and tack stores. Pick up the equine "shoppers news" in feed stores and go through their ads. If you have friends who are knowledgeable horse people, let them know you're in the market. If you are brave, you can also contact reputable horse dealers whose barns are well-established in their neighborhoods.

Reputable horse breeders, trainers, and dealers usually place their advertisements in the classifieds of horse magazines or specialty newspapers, or publications of a special breed or equine sport. Your local feed store will usually carry the issues of interest in your area.

All of these should give you a good list to work with.

The horses for sale at training stables are often in training with someone, and if you were to visit you could watch the horse in action. But many horses for sale are just standing around, for various reasons, waiting to be sold. This makes a big difference in selling methods. A horse that is not being ridden and is not useful to the owner is called, for obvious reasons, a "hayburner." Keep this definition in mind.

Once a person has decided to sell a horse, the sooner he sells it, the better. A horse has to be fed, even if he is not being ridden. One can advertise a dinette set or musical instruments for sale, and not spend anything (except for the ad) while waiting for the right buyer. A horse, on the other hand, is more expensive each day he's not sold. The seller has a very big incentive to find a buyer as soon as possible. Naturally the seller may be reluctant to tell a prospective buyer anything that might hinder the sale.

The seller doesn't *have* to tell anything about the horse that he doesn't want to. If the horse is of extreme age, has any bad habits, vices, or unsoundness, or has any other faults, the seller doesn't have to mention them. Of course if he is asked a specific question about the horse, he is supposed to answer truthfully, but he might not. He himself might be ignorant, or innocent, of the appropriate answer. What is a problem for one rider may not be a problem for the next rider at all. The opposite is true as well. The seller cannot guarantee what the horse will be like in a new rider's hands. The only thing he can be sure of is that once the horse is sold, the horse is the new owner's problem.

With your list in hand, you can phone the various people and ask for more information about the horse that was advertised. You can rule out a number of the ads with one call. Be sure to tell the dealer exactly what you are looking for—a horse for your novice-rider kid. Some of the dealers will tell you immediately that they don't have anything suitable right now, but might have later. You can give them your phone number and ask them to call you if something promising comes in. If a dealer knows what you want, he will keep you in mind while he is looking.

If the horse in the ad is a possibility, here are some of the things you should ask:

1. How long has the person had the horse? A horse that changes hands frequently may not be a good prospect.

2. Who rides him and how often? If a kid is riding him, ask how old the kid is.

3. What has the horse been used for?

4. Is he completely sound? Tell them you'll have a pre-purchase vet check if you do become interested, and the vet check will include drawing blood for testing.

5. Why is the horse for sale?

There are many possible answers. A sound reason that may lead to a good horse is, "owner going away to college." Just be sure the real owner really is going away to college. Another frequent reason given is a divorce settlement. This is a popular excuse and in some cases legitimate and can lead to a real bargain. For a smaller horse or pony, "sadly outgrown." You can tell when you see the horse and the owner if it's true that the owner has simply grown too big for that mount. If so, this might be a good possibility for your kid. "Too many horses" is a common situation that horse people get themselves into. However, they often keep the best horses for themselves.

If the horse belongs to someone else and is being sold "for a friend," the seller is probably in the dark about anything wrong with the horse, and he plans to stay in the dark. It's one way for both owner and seller to avoid being responsible for what the horse may do. You might want to avoid that horse.

You can learn a lot about the horse's suitability from the answers. There are two more important questions to ask.

6. Does the horse use a bit or a hackamore?"

The horse, to be suitable for a novice rider, should need only a mild bit. Even though you may not know one bit from another, you hope they will answer with either a short-shanked curb bit, or a plain snaffle, not a hackamore. A horse using a bit more severe than those, such as a twisted wire snaffle, probably means that the horse is not easy to control, or requires a more experienced rider. Later you can learn more about the different kinds of bits.

A hackamore is a type of bridle that has no bit in the horse's mouth at all. Young Western horses are often started in a hackamore by experienced trainers to prevent chance injury to a tender mouth from the bit. Young horses are unbalanced and it's easy for their mouths to get jerked if the horse is jumping around. The hackamore does not have any real punishing power, but controls the horse because the horse has been cleverly taught to believe that the hackamore does control him. Western horses may be shown in a Jaquima (hackamore) Class in a horse show if they are not more than five years of age, or not more than four years of age in the Junior Pleasure Division. A junior who is riding a four-year-old with a hackamore is no novice. As the horse learns to respond to a snaffle bit, which is put on underneath the hackamore at first, the trainer gradually dispenses with the hackamore.

In other words, a hackamore horse is usually one that is young and in training. It could also mean that you can't get a bit in the horse's mouth, or if you did, the horse would be too difficult to ride. This is not the kind of horse you should consider for your novice kid's first horse. You may meet someone who tells you a hackamore is good for a kid to use because the kid can't hurt the horse's mouth. That's only part of the story. Since your kid is not yet a skillful rider, she will be far better off with a horse that is controlled with a mild bit.

7. The other key question is, "Does the horse need a tie-down?"

You want the answer to be an absolute "No!" A tie-down, or standing martingale, is a leather strap that runs from the middle of the girth under the horse's belly to the nose-band of the bridle. It is a device to prevent the horse from throwing his head up too high. Head throwing is usually the result of the reins being constantly jerked by a poor rider; it's the horse's defense against injury.

Without the tie-down, that kind of horse can easily flip up his head and break his rider's nose, which is undesirable. A horse that needs a tie-down is definitely not suitable for a kid or a novice rider. In many horse show classes, martingales of any type are not permitted.

Perhaps you've wondered why the most reputable stables and their trainers advertise in horse magazines and specialty newspapers and seldom in the classified ads of the daily newspapers. That has an interesting explanation.

Chapter 15

The Used Car Salesman Syndrome, Or, How To Read The Classifieds

Caveat emptor. . . . discovering faults. . . . selling the less expensive horse. . . . public auctions. . . . classified ads . . . . examples and how to read them. . . . making an appointment.

There is one vital truth you should be aware of before you begin shopping for a horse. The Latin phrase, *caveat emptor*, "let the buyer beware," was never more true than in the case of the few people who have horses to sell but not a good reputation to maintain. It's up to the *buyer* to discover what faults the horse has, and the buyer has no recourse if he is stung.

There is a story of a man who bought a horse and was about to take him out on the trail when the horse lay down and refused to get up. Eventually the horse got up, but each time the man started for a ride, the horse lay down. The veterinarian came out and examined the horse thoroughly.

Bucking, cribbing, and rearing, are just a few of the vices that will cause a horse to be sold—and who would buy that horse if the seller were truthful?

"I don't know what's wrong, but I can tell you how to solve the problem," said the vet.

"How?" asked the anxious owner.

"The next time he's on his feet, sell him."

The vet may be fictional, but this story has some foundation in fact. The man probably bought the horse through a newspaper ad—and sold him the same way later.

The most common ways to sell the less expensive horses, especially hayburners, are (1) at a public auction, and (2) in the classified ads of the daily papers. All knowledgeable horsemen will agree on one thing—the auction is no place for a novice buyer.

The classifieds, unfortunately, are also a risky place for an inexperienced person to look for a horse, though not nearly as chancy as the auction. Ads in the newspapers can be very misleading, sometimes on purpose. Some people who are selling less expensive horses believe that they cannot afford to be completely honest or straightforward about the horse. These people usually advertise in the daily papers.

Many times perfectly honest horse people, especially families, advertise their horses for sale in the classified ads. But the reader of the ads, to avoid being disappointed, should have a thorough knowledge of horses and an understanding of the special equine terminology used.

The index to the classified section lists horses under such headings as, "Horses, Ponies, and Supplies." Ads ought to state the breed of horse (if known), sex, age, height, status of training, price, and something about the horse.

Here are some common abbreviations used in horse ads: m—mare (*not* male); g—gelding; s or stud—stallion; ch—chestnut; gr—grey; br—brown; blk—black. OBO—or best offer. QH—Quarter Horse; TB—Thoroughbred horse; Appy—Appaloosa horse; POA—Pony of the Americas; Conn.-Connemara pony; Shet.—Shetland pony; AQHA—horse registered with the American Quarter Horse Association.

y.o.—years old; h or h.h.—hands high. A hand is 4 inches, and a horse is always measured from ground level to the highest point of his withers—that big bump on top where his neck joins his body. The figure after the decimal point refers to inches, not tenths. A 15.2 hand horse is 15 × 4 = 60", plus 2", or 62" high at the withers.

The difference between a horse and a pony is the height. A horse measures more than 14.2 hands; a pony measures 14.2 hands or less. Certain breeds such as Quarter Horses and Arabians may have small horses that measure pony height but are considered horses for showing if they are registered. A pony can usually be shown in horse classes, but *no* horse can be shown in a pony class.

Let's look at a typical ad in a daily newspaper:

> Appy colt 1 yr Gentle, Flashy, halter broke. $350 obo

This ad *says* there is for sale a 1-year-old Appaloosa colt, not yet gelded, gentle, good-looking color markings, that can be haltered and led. The owner has stated a price but he'll take the best offer.

In addition to what the ad says, it *means* that whoever buys him will have to undertake the cost and risk of castrating the colt—having him gelded. The buyer will also have the expense of two years of feeding and caring for the colt without knowing what kind of riding horse he will turn out to be. The horse, when he is three years old, ought to be broken and trained by an expert. All of this involves a lot of expense with no return for a long time. Even then you don't know what kind of a horse you'll end up with. This is probably why he is for sale, and why the seller will entertain an offer lower than the asking price. As to whether or not the colt really is gentle, it's hard to say. Most stud colts (not yet gelded) are rather spunky and even with good ground manners would not be called gentle.

Here's another ad:

> Appy quarter mare, 6 y.o., 15., 1200 lbs., exp.rider $375 OBO

This ad says an Appaloosa-Quarter Horse cross, six-year-old mare, is 15. hands high (60" high at withers), weighs 1200 lbs., and needs an experienced rider.

What I would deduce from this ad is that here is a cross-bred mare who is not very tall but is quite heavy. She ought to be sensible and well-trained since she is now six years old, but she's not. In fact, she is so rank that she needs a very experienced rider to be able to handle her. To weigh that much at 15. hands means she is pretty fat, and I would guess that she hasn't been given enough exercise, probably because her owner is afraid to ride her.

Let's try another one:

> Registered Arab 6 y.o., breeding stock, bay $300 OBO

We can't tell from the ad if this is a stallion or mare or how tall it is, but it is six years old, has registration papers, and is a brown color with dark mane and tail. The person who submitted the ad doesn't know very much about horses because of all the things the ad does not tell you. When you see the words "breeding stock," it usually means the horse has never been trained to be ridden, or has been injured or is in some other way unsuitable for riding, but you could breed it if you wanted to. You have to wonder if anyone who knows so little about horses would have for sale a horse that was really good enough

for breeding stock, or is he for sale just because he isn't ridable.
Here's one that might be a good first horse for a kid:

Gelding, gentle, 15 yrs old. $250.

This horse is no particular breed and has no papers, but he's old
enough to be sensible. It's possible he is trail-wise and safe—a major
plus. A fifteen-year-old horse doesn't bring a high price, but sometimes
that's the easy-going kind of horse that would be fun for your kid to
ride. The horse may not be suitable for horse shows, but sometimes
that's not important for a kid's first horse.

You're beginning to get the picture, I'm sure.

Here's an ad from a horse magazine:

Bay TB g 16.3 h, 6 y.o., hunted 2 seasons by Master.
Bold and dependable. $5000.

This is a registered Thoroughbred 16.3 hands high (67" high at his
withers), a gelding, a very tall bay horse who is 6 years old and for
the past two years has been ridden for fox hunting by the Master of
the Hounds. The Master is usually a superb rider, and any horse that
has been hunted successfully by the Master should be quite handy in
jumping. Dependable means honest, that is, he would rather jump than
refuse a fence. If he has hunted he would probably be too strong for
a novice rider, but might be a good horse for a novice to move up to
later on.

Reading the Classifieds is an education in itself. There are always
some ads written purposely to mislead the innocent shopper.
Knowledgeable horse people find these ads a source of great amuse-
ment, but it's not funny if you're inexperienced and looking for a horse.
Here are a few of those phrases and what they could really mean:

"Always in the ribbons." This horse was shown in a small horse
show with less than five horses in each class. He placed last
each time but he got a ribbon.

"Easily trained." This horse doesn't know anything.

"Exceptional talent." Probably no brains.

"Loves to jump." Without a rider.

"Bold jumper." He rushes his fences.

"Bold mover." He likes to run away.

"Spirited." He's a devil to try to ride.

"Experienced on the show circuit." Maybe the rodeo?

"Green broke." A rider got on him once and then quit while he was ahead.

"Spirited but gentle." You can pat this horse and lead him around, but you may not be able to get on him.

"Gelded stallion." If his owner doesn't know the horse is really called a gelding, what does the horse know?

"Very athletic." Can buck up a storm.

"Flashy." Pretty to look at, but to ride???

"Started over fences." Someone jumped the horse over a couple of fences and then lost his nerve.

Actually most of those phrases are perfectly acceptable, legitimate descriptions of horses, if they appear in an ad by a reputable stable or trainer. When you make an appointment with a well-established trainer, it is important for you to be on time. Take along any willing, knowledgeable horseman and let him do most of the talking.

Unfortunately there are also disreputable trainers. If you are a novice looking for a horse, it's difficult to sort out fact from fiction. It takes a knowledgeable horseman to do that, or a determined and dedicated parent.

If the horse in the classified ad still sounds promising after you've talked to the owner, make an appointment to look at the horse, and don't be late. In fact, be early. At least half an hour early. Actually, you might want to show up the day before. I'll explain why.

Chapter 16

Look Around Before You Leap

Arriving early.... first visit.... reasons for drugging ....catching horse.... looking horse over.... the ideal horse.... someone else ride first.... test ride.... backyard kid's horse.... get help.

Suppose an ad in the newspaper sounds promising, and you've made an appointment for ten o'clock Saturday morning to see a horse at a stables out on Windy Lane. It will take you half an hour to get there.

Before you go, study the drawings at the back of the book of the parts of the horse, and the conformation. I suggest you photocopy the charts and take them with you. The people at the stable may get a charge out of that, but they should appreciate the fact that you're serious. It will certainly mark you as a novice, but you're not going to fool the seller anyway—don't try. You could carry copies for each horse you look at and make notes on the drawings. This will help you make a decision.

Your kid should be dressed in riding clothes in case she should ride the horse. If she has her own saddle, she should take it along, and also a clean saddle pad or a clean cloth to put under it. The owner himself might prefer to furnish the saddle pad; few horsemen want a chance skin ailment spreading from one horse to another.

On your way out to the stables, you're wondering what the horse will be like and if your kid should ride him and if she does, will she have any trouble with him.

While you are on your way to the stables, the owner is wondering what your kid is like, if she should ride the horse, and if she does, will she have any trouble with him.

A horse with good conformation is not only lovely to look at, but he is more likely to stay sound over a longer period of time.

The last thing the seller wants is trouble. The seller has no idea of the buyer's riding ability, but he does have to sell the horse. Probably the most common problem the seller has to face is knowing that the horse he is selling might be too much for the prospective buyer to handle. This is a risk he can't avoid.

To minimize the risk when someone comes to try out the horse, the seller has a simple solution – he can tranquilize the horse for a short period of time by injecting him with a common tranquilizer such as Acepromazine. A tranquilizer needs at least 15 minutes to take effect, and, depending on the dose and the horse, will last from half an hour to several hours. The horse will be quiet and easy to handle and the seller won't have to worry about the ability of whoever rides the horse – they'll get along just fine. Since Acepromazine is frequently used, tranquilizing a horse is commonly known as "aceing" the horse.

The problem is that the rider can't tell what the horse is really like if the horse has been "aced." She can see how he looks and moves and feel his gaits, but a very important thing, his temperament, remains hidden.

The easiest way for a buyer to prevent a horse being tranquilized is to show up very early to look at the horse, long before the seller expects him, so that the horse has not yet been given the drug. I suggest that the buyer appear at the stable at least half an hour before the appointed time, ask to see the horse, and then stay with the horse to be sure no one has a chance to give him a tranquilizer. To tranquilize a horse takes only a tiny syringe and a few seconds by an experienced horseman, injecting the drug in the muscles of the neck or rump. A skillful horseman can almost make it look as though he just slapped the horse fondly.

Unfortunately, another common reason for an owner to drug a horse is to hide a lameness. If the horse is feeling no pain, even an expert might find it impossible to spot a problem. Some pain medications take days to wear off, and only an examination by a vet can assess the situation.

So if your appointment at the stables on Windy Lane is at 10 o'clock in the morning, try being there by 9:15. Your kid won't mind a bit. If the horse is in a stall or paddock, she can spend the extra time patting the horse and talking to him and getting acquainted.

I can hear someone saying, "Oh, come on, people don't do that any more, that was back in the old days of horse traders. Ordinary people don't do that."

But ordinary people do. It happens more often than you think. Time after time I hear of a family who bought a horse that had been tried out several times, and he was fine – until they got the horse home. Horses, like children, act differently in different environments, but if the horse goes bananas and is a nervous wreck after he's unloaded at his new home, you know perfectly well he was aced at the stable each time the kid tried him out.

Or when the kid got the horse home, the horse limped. When asked, the former owner said the horse was probably hurt in the trailer and he'd be all right in a couple of days. He never did get over it. Again, the horse was probably drugged to mask the unsoundness when he was ridden. With caution and care, you can avoid a situation like that.

If you have reason to suspect that somehow the horse has been tranquilized in spite of your precautions, try going to the stables to see the horse some day when you do not have an appointment. If the owner doesn't want you to see the horse or have him brought out, you'll know there's something wrong. The sure way to learn if a horse has been drugged is to have the vet make a blood and urine test during the pre-purchase vet check. It will help to let the horse seller know that you intend to have the vet draw blood for a test before you finalize the sale.

The owner of a horse that is really good for kids will not tranquilize his horse because he doesn't need to. He knows he's not taking much of a risk.

When you first make the appointment you might ask the seller not to have the horse already caught and saddled, you want your kid to be the one to catch the horse. If the horse is hard to catch, you should learn about it now.

When you arrive at the stables, hunt up the man with whom you have the appointment. Depending on the situation, you can figure out how to visit the horse right away and stay with him. If the horse is in a stall or paddock by himself, the owner might let your kid catch the horse, tie him up, and start brushing him. She'll learn something about his ground manners while she's doing that. If the horse is in a corral or pasture with other horses, you kid might be a little timid about going in there to catch the horse. Perhaps she can ask the person who goes to catch the horse if she can go along. You can see what the horse is like when it's time to catch him.

When the horse is caught, have the stablehand lead the horse out and stand him sideways to you so you can get a good look at the whole horse. If you don't have an experienced horseman with you, the next steps aren't going to be easy. As a non-horse person, you can take out the drawing on conformation and try to compare it with the real horse in front of you. Keep in mind that the perfect horse doesn't exist, and standards are slightly different for different breeds. The following description is intended to give you, in the absence of an expert, a picture of the kind of horse you would like to find for your kid. *But appearance is not as important as his disposition and age and training.*

The ideal horse is attractive to look at, is alert, stands four-square, and gives the appearance of being in good proportion. That is, he should look as though all his parts fit together well.

The neck should be of moderate length, thick at the base where it joins the body, and slender at the throat latch where the neck joins the head, carried high and slightly arched.

The back should be moderate to short, strong and well-muscled, and the croup should be the same height as, or slightly lower than, the withers.

The hindquarters should be wide and well-muscled. You should see a straight line from the point of the horse's buttocks through the hock to the back of the fetlock.

The chest should be large, wide, and deep. The line of the shoulder should form a 45-degree angle with the ground line.

The forelegs should be well-muscled with cannon bones shorter than the forearms.

The pastern joints should be of moderate to long length, sloping at a 45-degree angle from the ground.

The withers should be well-defined. Too high may push the saddle back from where it is supposed to be; too low may let the saddle slip forward.

The hooves should be in good proportion to the size of the horse, clean and well-formed, an even shape, and without cracks running up the hooves.

The head should be in proportion to the rest of the horse, be carried well, have bright eyes that are large and set well apart, a broad forehead, medium or small ears that are active and set apart on the head, and a refined muzzle that has a chiseled look.

Next study the horse from the front and the rear. His legs should be straight and square to the ground, set moderately apart with some width for the chest in front, and the feet large and wide at the heels.

Sometimes a first look at a horse turns you off completely. You don't care for him and you know you're not going to buy him. He's—too big, too small, just doesn't have the right look in his eye, or whatever. You will do everyone a favor to let the seller know right away so no more of his time is wasted. Try to tell the seller tactfully that the horse isn't quite what you had in mind. "Big, but not that big." Or, "small, but not that small." But don't criticize the horse. Even if you think he is ugly you might give him a chance, especially if your kid is young and very much a beginner. Beauty is as beauty does, and a kind horse who loves children and takes care of them is absolutely beautiful, no matter what his appearance.

There is one other thing I would check. Ask the man handling the horse to open the horse's mouth so you can see the horse's incisors— the front teeth. The more yellow and slanted the front teeth, the older the horse, but the horse's age is not what you're interested in right now. You will have the vet check his teeth if the horse is a good possibility.

See if the flat surfaces of the horse's upper and lower incisors meet squarely, and the front of the incisors are not worn off more than the back. If the front edges of the teeth are worn off so upper and lower teeth do not meet, the horse is what we call a "cribber." Cribbing or wind-sucking is a stable vice often begun through boredom. It consists of the horse fastening his teeth around an object like a rail and sucking in air, then belching it back out. A cribber is not only unpleasant to have around, he is very difficult to keep in good condition because his belly is full of air. There are times when owning a cribber is worth all the pain, but not when you are looking for your kid's first horse.

If the horse is a possibility, you should ask for the horse to be "jogged out" for you and your kid to look at. Jogging out means someone taking the haltered horse by the lead rope and making him trot or jog in a straight line *with the lead rope slack* while you watch the movement of the horse's head and legs. If the lead rope is slack, the horse can move his head as he needs to, and this is important.

By this time you probably have learned what a horse's gaits are. In case you're unclear, turn to Chapter 20.

At the walk and at the canter or lope, the horse's head moves up and down in even rhythm because his head acts as a balance for his body. But when the horse is trotting or jogging, the head is absolutely steady and maintains the same position while the rest of the body goes up and down. If a horse is slightly lame in one leg, it will show up at the trot by his head bobbing or nodding to alter his stride and cut down on the pain of impact by the lame leg. This is why the trot is called the diagnostic gait. A lame horse may appear sound at the walk, but he can not appear sound at the trot unless he has been drugged and is feeling no pain.

The horse should first be walked straight away from you, turned, and be walked straight back so you can see how he moves. Then he should be trotted or jogged the same way.

His walk should be with long easy steps in rhythm, his legs moving forward in a straight line with his feet lifted up off the ground and put down in an even four beats. His head should move up and down in rhythm with the footfalls. His hind feet should not be wide apart as he moves. You don't want to see his front feet "flapping" out or in, called winging or dishing. Winging is not as bad a fault as dishing; in the latter the horse may strike one foot with another and injure himself.

If the horse is going to be ridden Western, his jog should be a very smooth, two-beat gait with not much elevation in his steps so the rider

Some horses have really funny ways of going. Instead of moving straight, their feet can wing or dish—the legs seem to flap in or out, or one foot will strike another while walking. These things can often lead to lameness.

can sit the jog comfortably without bouncing. If the horse is going to be ridden under English tack, his trot should be even but springy with knees and hocks well-flexed in two-beat rhythm, giving the impression of lightness and elegance. Western or English, his head should be held steady and not move up and down at the trot.

There are a lot of things a potential buyer should watch for besides winging and dishing, but a non-horse person cannot be expected to pass judgment on those.

If the horse seems sound and quiet enough, tell the seller you'd like to see the horse ridden by someone else while you watch. Ask the seller if your kid could help groom the horse and get him ready for riding. If your kid is scared of the horse, now is the time to find out so you can leave gracefully.

If you are both happy about the way the horse performs under saddle with another rider, then your kid can finally mount up and try him out on her own in an enclosed arena. Your kid should walk him around to get the feel, then trot or jog him, and practice starting and stopping. If she's sufficiently advanced to put him in a slow canter or a lope, let her try it. If the seller knows the horse well, he might make some helpful suggestions at this point.

Fifteen to twenty minutes for the first ride will probably be enough for you to know if your kid can get along with him, and if the horse is still a possibility. Have your kid dismount and with the owner's permission put the horse away. And then make another appointment to try out the horse a second time. Three tryouts is even better.

The owner might tell you he has other interested parties coming to try out the horse, which may or may not be true. You'll have to decide which course to follow, but don't be pressured into hasty decisions. There will always be more horses. Surely your kid should try four or five horses before choosing one even if you think you have struck gold soon after beginning the search. Don't forget that the horse you choose is going to become a member of your family.

Looking at a kid's horse kept in his own backyard is somewhat different from looking at a horse for sale by a dealer. A family who for whatever reason must sell their kid's backyard horse is often more concerned over finding a good home for the horse than in getting their money's worth. Sometimes the ad reads, "to good home only." You want to be sure that the horse is suitable for your kid; they want to be assured that your kid is suitable for the horse.

It's refreshing to deal with people who care a lot about their horse, but it doesn't necessarily follow that the horse will be suitable for your kid. The horse may have been allowed by his young owner to develop bad habits, especially if the owner hasn't been taking regular lessons.

Try to be as objective and careful as you are with a horse from a big stable. You can still follow the guidelines above for arriving earlier than planned, as a precautionary measure.

Another word of caution. The kind of horse you buy should depend largely on how well your kid is riding, *right now*. A frequent mistake

A horse that's really good for kids is a treasure and needs no tranquilizers. Jodie's father saw this Shetland pony, Boots, being ridden by some kids along a road, followed the pony home, and persuaded the family to sell him. Boots lets all the kids ride him.

parents make is buying a horse for the future rather than the present. They want the kid to "grow with the horse." It doesn't work that way. She needs a horse that is already grown and is sensible, and she will grow because of what he can teach her. Whatever the level your kid is riding, she needs a horse she can ride without fear *today*. Outgrowing a horse, like growing up, will take care of itself when the time comes.

When you think you have narrowed the field of possible horses to one or two whom you like a lot, then is the time to have a professional horseman or knowledgeable friend, if one is available, come to watch your kid ride the horse before you make an offer for the horse or spend the money for a pre-purchase vet check. If no expert horseman is at hand, you will have to depend completely on the veterinarian to help you. You can trust him; he knows what he's doing.

If you are sure that a certain horse is the one you would like to buy, then comes the hard part—coming to an agreement, and it's not just about price.

Chapter 17

Closing The Deal

Agreements of sale....trial period....contingencies ....down payment....price according to seasons.... pre-purchase vet exam....conducting the exam.... bringing the horse home.

Whatever arrangements you make for buying a horse, put them all down in writing. Anything that the seller tells you about the horse should be in black and white on a piece of paper. This includes any statements about the horse's history, suitability, performance, and soundness, what he eats and how much and if he has any idiosyncrasies about his feed. If the seller is unwilling to sign the statement, you will be better off not dealing with him.

Before you sign the final agreement to buy the horse, make sure that the deal is contingent upon a satisfactory pre-purchase vet check. The horse won't speak out; the seller won't speak out; only the veterinarian after a careful examination of the horse can tell you certain things you need to know. Experienced horsemen always have a potential mount examined by a vet. You will need all the help you can get, so put the vet-check at the top of your list, even if the exam costs more than the horse. It is an investment in your kid's safety, and insurance for the expense and TLC your family will invest in that horse over the many years ahead.

It is highly desirable to have the horse for a trial period if the seller will agree. The ideal arrangement is for your kid to ride the horse for at least a week in the new surroundings where the horse is to be kept—to see if the horse is really what you think he is. Some horses can be very calm in their own barns, but when moved to a strange place come unglued and are difficult to handle.

At the time that you make your offer, tell the owner you would like your kid to try out the horse "at home" before the deal becomes final. If the horse is truly what the owner has said he is, and is not an expensive animal, usually the owner will say yes to a trial. Two weeks is better than one, and may be granted when the owner is reasonably sure the kid will be so happy with the horse that her parents will buy it.

If the horse is a well-trained expensive show animal, the owner has to exercise considerable judgment about a trial period. It doesn't take long for a green rider to ruin a good horse. If the owner knows the stable where the horse will be going, and if he has confidence in the instructor under whom your kid is riding, he might be willing to let the horse go for a trial.

If the seller agrees to a trial period, you may:

1. Give a check for payment (in part or in full as agreed) to the seller which he is to hold until the date you both have agreed upon for the trial period. Post-dated checks are not legal; have the seller sign a statement that he will hold the check. At the end of that time, if you and your kid like the horse, you'll keep the horse and the seller will cash the check. If your kid decides before the time is up that she does not like the horse, you return the horse and the seller returns the check.

2. Sign a statement and give it to the seller saying that you will take complete responsibility for the horse and will return him in the same condition in which you received him if you decide not to buy him.

It is also a good idea for you to consider taking out mortality insurance on an expensive horse for the time the horse is on trial. Most horse magazines carry ads for equine insurance.

If the seller will not let the horse go for trial, you should make a down-payment and write out, for the seller to sign, a statement that the final payment is contingent upon a satisfactory pre-purchase vet check. Ask the seller for a signed statement in which he guarantees the horse to be suitable for a certain purpose (a jumper, a trail horse, etc.) with a description of the horse as the seller has said it is. If the horse does not pass the vet check, the down payment will be returned to you. If the horse passes the vet check but if for any reason you decide not to go through with the deal, the down payment is not returned to you; you lose it.

This sample is a guideline for a basic contract of sale. When in doubt, talk to an attorney.

Tentative Contract for Purchase of a Horse

On this date _____, [name of seller], hereinafter referred to as Seller, agrees to sell to [name of buyer], hereinafter referred to as Buyer, and Buyer agrees to purchase the horse known as [registered name if available], Registration Number _____, described as [color and markings, size, and sex], foaled _____, which Seller warrants to be in good health and to which Seller has clear title. Buyer agrees to pay to Seller the total purchase price of $_____ with a (non-refundable) down-payment of $_____ (down payment may be given to a Third Party to hold) paid by Check No. _____ upon signing this agreement, the balance of $_____ to be paid (10 days hence, or date given) (1) contingent upon a satisfactory pre-purchase veterinary examination by a licensed veterinarian of the Buyer's choosing and expense and (2) provided that the Buyer finds the animal suitable for his purposes, the horse's registration papers to be delivered (with the horse, or upon final payment).

Seller warrants the animal to be represented as follows:

[Full description]

(Date) _____ Signed _____
                                              (Seller)
                               Signed _____
                                              (Buyer)

IT IS BEST TO CHECK WITH YOUR ATTORNEY.

At this point you'll say, "But you haven't mentioned anything about the price." The reason is that the terms of the agreement are much more difficult to settle; deciding on the price is easy by contrast.

If the price being asked for the horse in which you are interested is listed as "firm," it means just that, and you can forget about bargaining. You can decide whether or not you want to pay that price. If the price is not marked "firm," you can make a tentative offer that seems reasonable to you without insulting the seller, and hope he'll accept it, or come back with a price in between yours and his.

Prices for horses vary during the year according to the season. In the spring, around Memorial Day, the market is at its highest. That's when people are buying horses to ride all summer. In the fall, around Labor Day, the market usually drops. In most parts of the United States, people don't ride as much in winter as in summer. If they don't want the expense of maintaining a horse over the winter, they'll put the horse up for sale and usually will accept any reasonable offer.

During the summer, saddle horses are in great demand at resorts, camps, and vacation back-packing places. With the approach of winter, the owner will put the horses out to pasture or sell them and plan to pick up new ones the following spring. Keep the seasons in mind when you are making your offer.

Once you and the seller have agreed on the price, *you* phone the vet of your choice for an appointment. If the seller says *you don't need a vet check* because he just had one performed on the horse and he'll give you the certificate, tell him thanks but no thanks. You can't tell when the vet check was done or for what reason. The seller probably knows something that he doesn't want you to find out. You'll save money by dropping that prospect from your list.

Be sure it is you and not the seller who hires the vet. Do not ask the seller to recommend a vet, or use a vet in the seller's local area. If it's too far for the vet you have chosen to come to the barn, you should have the horse trailered to that vet or to a clinic out of the area so that the horse will be examined by a vet who has no loyalty to the seller. You will have to pay the trailering expenses but it will be worth it to get an unbiased opinion. If anything should happen to the horse on the trip, he belongs to you at the price you've agreed upon.

With luck, the vet you want will come. You want him to examine the horse when you and your kid will be there, and, if you can arrange it, *the owner and seller will not.*

The vet is there to criticize the horse and the seller naturally would try to defend the horse. The purpose of the vet check is to discover any faults or weaknesses that might keep the horse from being suitable for your kid. The vet doesn't want anyone around to try to make light of his findings or to say something like, "Oh, he's had that for years and it's never bothered him." You are paying for the vet and it will pay you to listen to what he has to say. The vet's primary goal is to check out the horse's health and soundness and give you an honest report.

First of all, the vet will want to talk with you about what kind of a horse you are looking for, what kind of riding your kid wants to do, and how well you know the horse he is going to look at. The kind of riding is vital because a horse that is suitable for trail riding or equitation classes, might not hold up for Eventing or barrell racing. A horse that cannot take the stress of jumper classes may be able to handle hunter classes because there aren't as many fences and they are lower. The vet will examine the horse to see if he is suitably sound for the use to which he will be put.

Secondly, give the vet the written statement signed by the seller giving certain facts about the horse and recount for the vet as much of the history of the horse as you got from the seller. During the examination, the vet will check to see if the horse he is looking at matches the description given by the seller.

You would be surprised at some of the "mistakes" that are made. In one case the buyer showed the registration papers of the horse to prove the horse was eight years old when the vet knew from the horse's teeth the horse had to be a lot older than eight.

The papers were in beautiful order—too beautiful. On the reverse side of the registration papers was a diagram of the horse on which all the markings of the horse were recorded for identification. Someone had beautifully colored in the horse's markings on the diagram, and the colored picture was exactly like the horse. The problem was that the coloring didn't match the original registered markings underneath the black and white. The horse that was being vetted was about 15 years old.

Or the seller can swear that the horse was never on the racetrack, but the vet finds the tattoo number of the horse's upper lip—a requirement for entry on the track.

If a seller is lying about one thing, he could be lying about everything else. *Caveat emptor.*

The vet is not there to certify the disposition and temperament of the horse, but they become evident to the vet as he works around the horse. His opinion is invaluable. Each vet has his own method of conducting a pre-purchase exam, so I can only give you a general idea of its procedure.

A vet usually begins his examination with the horse's head. The vet will probably want to start with the horse inside the barn so he can examine the eyes. He will look into the horse's eyes with his ophthalmoscope for any abnormality in the cornea or lens that causes blindness. He will look over the head for fractures (horses can run into things), sinus infections, pharyngeal problems, and any other respiratory ailments that could cause difficulty in breathing. He will check the mouth to see if the incisors meet squarely and that the molars are not sharp or irregularly worn. He will be able to give you an approximation of the horse's age by examination of the incisors.

He will check the heart, the lungs, listen to the gut sounds, and look over the skin for lesions. He will take the horse's temperature and check the pulse and respiration rates. He will examine the ligaments of the neck, the cervical vertebrae, the groin area and the genitals. All these things are indicators of the animal's health.

He will ascertain that a gelding was properly castrated. If he was not, the gelding can act like a stallion, and your kid would be in for a lot of trouble.

If the horse is a mare, the vet should check to see if she is pregnant. The last thing you want your kid to own is a pregnant mare. To horse owners not in the breeding business, a pregnant mare is bad news—a lot of expense and time off for the mare when she cannot be ridden, plus the extra care, expense, and training needed for the foal as it grows up. The owner's easy way out is to sell the mare while the owner can still claim she just has a hay belly.

No, you can't tell by looking at the mare. A young Thoroughbred filly was making a good record for herself on the racetrack and the owners had high hopes for her. One day she did not race well at all, and the owners were shocked that evening when she gave birth to a colt. Of course *someone* knew she had gotten out and gotten bred, but whoever that was would have lost his job had he told. Both mother and son were okay, but if all the people that worked with and watched that filly for months didn't know she was pregnant, how can an amateur expect to know?

The next part of the vet's examination is concentrated on conformation and soundness. The horse you are interested in for your kid should be at least eight years old. An eight-year-old automobile will have some dings and dents in it, and so may an eight-year-old horse. The vet will decide which ones are just blemishes that are unsightly but harmless, and which ones may cause trouble, or constitute an unsoundness.

He will stand the horse outside, probably put on chaps, and examine each leg and foot in turn. The vet might start at the body and work his way down one leg, palpating the joints, tendons, and ligaments. He will be watching for swelling or heat or tender places. He will test the digital pulse in the feet. At the foot he will look for uneven wearing of the hooves and tell-tale rings that mean a history of laminitis or inflammation of the hooves. With his hoof testers and a knife he will check for any abcesses, contracted heels, corns, bruises, etc., and dropped soles. Then he will work his way up the leg again. Some of the things which could show up are sidebones, ringbone, osselets, wind puffs, splints, bowed tendons, swollen knees, capped elbow, capped hock, spavin, and thoroughpin. These aren't all of the things the vet could find, but they are the most common ones.

When he has finished the four legs, the vet will have his assistant walk the horse in a straight line, trot him, and finally lunge him in a small circle on a hard surface, both ways, in all three gaits. Last of all, he will hold up in turn each of the horse's legs in a flexed position for a minute or so, and then let go and have his assistant jog out the horse immediately afterward. If there is an "iffy" soreness it will probably show up right then.

In the case of a rather expensive horse, sometimes the vet may recommend radiography (x-rays) for a questionable area.

You can see why a vet check is indeed a *must*.

If there is any question in your mind about the horse's being drugged for any reason, the vet should take urine and blood samples for analysis. The actual tests don't have to be made, but once the blood is drawn and frozen it will be available for testing if a question arises.

Some sellers can be extremely clever when it comes to drugging a horse. In one instance a horse was sold with a down payment and 30 days to pay. In the meantime the buyer took the horse home and rode him very happily. The former owner came by every day to see the horse and check on how he was getting along. At least that's what the buyer thought. Two days after the debt was paid off and the seller no longer came to see the horse every day, the horse went permanently lame. They never could be sure what kind of medication the seller had used to disguise the lameness.

When the vet has finished his examination, he should give you his report in writing. If the horse does pass the vet check and your family is on its way to owning a horse, ask the vet if he thinks anything about the horse's present diet and shoeing should be changed. If so, write down his instructions, and use them for guidelines when the horse is at his new home.

Make the final arrangements with the seller for completed purchase, bill of sale, and delivery, buy the good hay and other feed if the horse will be kept in yours or someone else's backyard, and double-check your list of tack and clothing for your kid and her horse.

From the vet's written report, copy down the horse's normal pulse, respiration rate, and temperature. These three vital signs are called "PRT," and you will want to record those figures later on the horse's "I.D." card. The card will describe the horse and his habits, and will prove very useful.

Take a 3x5 index card and if your kid prints clearly, have her fill it out as shown in the diagram. If someone might have trouble deciphering her printing, perhaps you should help. Write down the horse's barn name (nickname) and description such as breed, height, age, and sex, his color and markings. If ever the horse should escape from his stable, a complete description is immediately available for whoever has to look for the horse.

Write down any vices he might have that you know of (let's hope he doesn't have any), and leave space for any allergies as you learn about them, such as reaction to a certain medication, or brand of fly spray. Then write down his menu—what kind of hay and the supplements

---

HORSE'S NAME   **PERSON**

HEIGHT   **BREED**   **DATE FOALED**   **SEX**

COLOR AND MARKINGS

VICES:

ALLERGIES:

DIET: AM:

     NOON:

     PM:

PULSE   **RESPIRATION**   **TEMPERATURE**

The horse's I.D. card

Commander's Choice "Captain"   Bill Wilbur

15.1 hh   QH   8-10-83   Gelding

Golden Buckskin, Black points; Star, snip,

Left hind and left fore - half stockings

VICES: None

ALLERGIES: None

DIET: AM: 8 lbs oat hay

    NOON: 2 lbs barley if worked

    PM: 10 lbs alfalfa

PULSE: 36   RESPIRATION: 12   TEMPERATURE: 99°

Sample of completed I.D. card

he gets, how much, and when. When someone else has to feed the horse, the necessary information is there in black and white.

Last of all, record the horse's pulse, respiration rate, and temperature, or PRT. If later the horse acts as though he might be sick, taking his PRT to compare with his normal rate before you phone the vet will give the vet a lot more to go on in deciding how serious the problem is. When the I.D. card is properly filled out, your kid should put it in a plastic envelope and post it in the barn outside the horse's stall or paddock, or better still, next to the peg where the horse's halter is hung.

When you have taken care of all these details, you are ready to have the horse brought to his new home. A horse familiar with horse shows and other barns may not get upset at all at being moved. But a horse who hasn't been around very much might be like a kid in a new neighborhood—scared.

Give the horse time to get used to the place before your kid starts riding him. It's good for your kid to hand-walk the horse all around the new place. If he's going to be in a pasture, she should lead the horse around to show him the boundaries, the location of the water, his shelter, and where he will be fed. Some fresh hay will help convince the horse that he's moved to a good home. Your kid can talk to him without bothering him while he's eating. The next day she can tie him up and groom him, then hand-walk him again if he still seems a little nervous. When he is relaxed and settled down, your kid can start riding him.

You may have noticed earlier when I listed the qualities that make a horse suitable for a kid, I didn't mention any particular breed or color or sex of the horse. We'll talk about that next.

Chapter 18

Four Wheel Drive or Cadillac?

Importance of color, breed, sex....definitions....
Ponies: Shetland, POA, Welsh, Connemara, Quarter
Pony and crosses....Horses: Quarter Horse, Morgan,
cross-breds and grade horses....matching horse and
rider.

When we made a list of the qualifications of a horse suitable for your kid, the color, breed, and gender were conspicuously absent from that list, and with good reason. Those three factors are non-essential in determining a horse's suitability for a novice rider.

We mentioned breed in an earlier chapter. A breed of horses has a common origin and certain characteristics that are transmitted consistently to the offspring, by which each member of that breed can be identified.

Horses don't all look alike. As you get to know a breed, you will be able to pick out members of that breed from a large herd because of certain characteristics.

In foreign countries known for certain breeds of horses, their governments are responsible for breeding records and registration of the horses. In the United States anyone can start a breed association.

A breed registration association is a group of people who form an organization to keep records of their horses' bloodlines and promote that breed. Some breed societies are hundreds of years old; others were begun very recently.

Breeds range from the diminutive Shetland pony to the sleek and shining Thoroughbred, from the compact and dependable Quarter Horse to the poetry-in-motion white Lipizzaners of the Spanish Riding School in Vienna.

A few breed associations are based on the color of the horse rather than purity of bloodlines or conformation. Examples of color breeds are the Appaloosa, Buckskin, and Palomino. Those horses must exhibit certain colors and markings or they cannot be registered in that "breed." The Pinto Horse Association of America registers horses and ponies of any type and breed as long as they are multicolored.

Margaret, 12, on her 16-year-old Appaloosa, Rex, finds Trail Horse classes a breeze.

The American Paint Horse Association is a combination of bloodline and color. It registers only those multicolored horses which have the breeding of Quarter Horses and Thoroughbreds with primarily a stock horse conformation.

If a buyer's heart is set upon a certain color, he is seriously handicapping himself in his selection of a horse. Many experienced horsemen like to point out that you can't ride a color. In looking for a kid's horse, color is the *least* important factor. There's a world of truth in the old saying, "A good horse is never a bad color." There are individual horses with good dispositions for children in almost every breed, but the wisest approach is to try to be color blind when you begin your search.

The main purpose of registration is (1) to increase the value of the horse for breeding, (2) to make him eligible for certain types of racing, or (3) to make him eligible for competitions restricted to that particular breed.

If you should ask, "What is the best breed?" the answer is, "It depends entirely on what you plan to do with the horse." Some breeds are more adaptable than others to certain uses. Quarter Horses are well-known for pleasure riding and stock horse work; Thoroughbreds are adept at jumping and dressage; Arabians have gained fame in endurance riding. Brilliant performances in all disciplines have been shown by horses of mixed breeds and of unknown parentage.

Horses with Arabian or Thoroughbred blood in them are called "hot-blooded" because they are hot and high-strung in comparison with the phlegmatic cold-blooded draft or pulling horses. If you combine

11-year-old Mandy enjoys entering her Paint Horse, Junior, in the 4-H horse shows.

hot blood with cold blood you get, guess what, Warmblooded horses. Registered Warmblood breeds from Europe have become very popular in the United States. In many shows you will see Warmbloods such as Hanoverians, Trakheners, Westphalians, Dutch Warmbloods, and Swedish Warmbloods. These breeds have maintained strict breeding standards and records for hundreds of years. A fairly recent breed is the Danish Warmblood. Originally developed for cavalry mounts and carriage horses, Warmbloods are now bred primarily for dressage, but many are superb jumpers.

Breeders are constantly experimenting with crossing established breeds to develop new ones. Today you will see cross-breds (each parent registered but not in the same breed), and grade horses (offspring of one registered parent and a non-registered parent), and scrubs (of totally unknown parentage), also known as "horse horses." It is common nowadays to use "grade horses" to denote any horse or pony without a pedigree. A friend of ours has an Event horse of mixed parentage stabled in Burbank, Calif., whom she fondly refers to as her Burbank Warmblood or Kinairdly. You kinairdly tell what breeds are in his bloodline.

A breed can be known for a certain disposition and temperament, but always there are exceptions within each breed. Quarter Horses are supposed to be quiet, lacking the fire necessary for higher levels of dressage, but a number of Quarter Horses have gained reknown through their brilliant performances in Grand Prix dressage.

Thoroughbreds are supposed to be nervous and rather high-strung. A friend of mine with a shattered right ankle due to an accident off the horse, had to use her Thoroughbred ex-racehorse as a crutch to get to a tree stump where he stood quietly for 15 minutes while she climbed painfully hand-over-hand into the saddle and let him carry her carefully home.

Within each breed there is such a variety that you must never forget it is the individual horse that you are considering for your kid, but a breed can be a starting point.

We haven't mentioned gender for your kid's horse. Stallions are definitely unsuitable for kids. The American Horse Shows Association wisely bars Juniors from exhibiting stallions except under certain very limited circumstances. The choice is between geldings and mares. Geldings are usually more reliable and emotionally stable. Mares are often more trusting and exhibit maternal instincts, but when they are in heat they can be unpredictable. Yet there are unreliable geldings, and very steady mares. Again, deal with the individual horse and let your kid see how well she gets along with that particular gelding or mare.

If your riding instructor, 4-H leader, or Pony Club instructor is assisting you, or if you have secured some kind of professional help in looking for and choosing a horse, I shall assume that the professional will try to see that you purchase the right kind of horse for your kid.

But if you are beyond help, geographically speaking, and your kid is going to be on her own without lessons, it is imperative that you find a horse that is reliable and easy for her to handle. *Buying a horse for a kid who will have no instruction requires a different kind of horse from one with whom the kid will have close supervision.* If she is taking lessons, her instructor will teach her how to take care of the horse. If she is on her own, she needs a horse that will take care of *her.*

If your kid is small, you might consider a pony instead of a horse. Ponies are small in size but can be big in courage and performance. In the 1930's, a 13.2 Connemara pony of the Irish Jumping Team won the Open Jumper Class at Madison Square Gardens against big horses. Seldom Seen, a 14.3 Connemara/Thoroughbred cross, surprised everyone but his rider by becoming a Grand Prix Champion in dressage.

Some kids who are intimidated by the size of a horse can enjoy taking care of and riding a gentle and well-trained pony. A youthful owner who gives a well-trained pony kindness and love will find that the pony repays her with a devotion and dedication that would astonish some adult horsemen.

The problem is finding a pony that is indeed well-trained and good-natured. Unfortunately, not all ponies are sweet and gentle. A very small pony frequently is not a suitable mount for a child. If the pony is too small to be ridden by a competent adult, often his training is neglected or put into the hands of a child to "train." Such a pony can not only be frightening but dangerous. A bad experience with that kind of pony can destroy a kid's love of horses.

Although finding a truly reliable pony is a difficult task, it is worth the effort. A good pony can be a great teacher and confidence-builder. Many of the members of our U.S. Equestrian Teams began their riding careers on ponies.

There are three distinct advantages to learning to ride on a good pony.

(1) A kid can manage a pony her own size much better than she can a full-size horse.

(2) Any kid who learns to ride a pony with its short quick stride and, in some cases, a certain amount of unpredictability, is usually capable of riding almost any kind of horse as she grows older.

(3) When the kid does fall off, she doesn't have far to fall.

A pony measures not more than 14.2 hands, and has a distinct conformation which distinguishes him from small horses. There are a great

Piper, Sasha, and Lee are rewarding the Connemara pony, Dr. Pepper, with an apple after a successful lesson.

many pony breeds around the world, but the four most common and agreeable breeds of ponies in the United States are the Connemara, Pony of the Americas, Shetland, and Welsh. A recent addition to the pony ranks is the American Quarter Pony, small registered Quarter Horses who are technically pony size. The imported Norwegian Fjord Pony is also becoming popular. To obtain additional information on these and on other pony breeds, check the Resource Guide. If you want to see a fascinating variety of all sizes, shapes, and colors of ponies in action, being jumped and ridden English and Western, go to a pony show! It is a spectacle you will not likely forget.

The smallest pony of all is the Shetland pony, a very old breed from the Shetland Islands in Great Britain. The Islands, forty miles north of Scotland, are noted for their harsh climate, and consequently Shetlands have great stamina and are extremely hardy when not overfed.

Shetland ponies now come in three types. There is the original or miniature draft-horse type, the road-type pony which through selective breeding is a more refined and spirited pony with long neck and fine bone, and the older type of Shetland, called the Classic American Shetland. The latter is rapidly regaining popularity. The pony must not be over 46" or 11.2 hands to be registered in the American Shetland

Pony Stud Book. Most are 43" or 10.4 hands and under.

Most Shetlands in regular horse shows in the U.S. are the road-type Shetland, shown under harness with two- or four-wheeled vehicles. It is much easier to train a Shetland for harness than for riding because of its diminutive size. But the Classic American Shetland is increasingly making its appearance in shows. At Pony Club Rallies I have seen small Shetlands with very small riders performing dressage tests with great enthusiasm, the ponies obviously enjoying competing against big horses.

A Shetland pony should have a small head with large wide-spread eyes and small ears, sloping shoulders and good withers, a compact body with strong legs, and a very full mane and tail. Shetlands if well cared for live long and useful lives, some still working at thirty or more years of age. They can be any color, even pinto.

The grade Shetland pony, Surprise, is only 38" high and has been outgrown by Steve but he's just right for Laura and Rebecca.

A pairs class is lots of fun for these ten-year-old girls on their great ponies, Kathy on the Connemara Tralee and Julie on the POA Popover.

Slightly larger than the Shetland is a newly developed breed called the Pony of the Americas, or POA. POAs were developed here in America as a miniature combination of the Arabian and Quarter Horse conformation with Appaloosa coloring.

The foundation sire of the POA was a black-and-white leopard-spotted stallion, Black Hand, by a black Shetland pony out of an Appaloosa mare. A number of breeds contributed to the development of the POA. Among them are Welsh and Hackney ponies and a prepotent stallion with Arab conformation from a band of Mexican mustangs in the Sierra Madre mountains in Mexico. It is generally believed that those mustangs were descended from Spanish Barb horses brought to America by the Conquistadores.

Because of the variety of bloodlines and the care in breeding to produce a pony especially suitable for children, in size and disposition, the POA is an excellent mount for a kid too large for a Shetland pony, but not yet ready for a horse. The POA ranges in size from 46" to 56" or 11.2 hands to 14. hands.

The POA head may have a slightly concave face like an Arab. The eyes are large and the neck is slightly arched with prominent withers. The body is short-coupled and strong, and has free movement with long strides. The POA is an all-around pleasure and performance pony, popular because they are easy to train and usually have a gentle and sensible disposition. If a POA offspring does not have the Appaloosa coloring, he cannot be registered, but he can still be an ideal mount for a kid.

An ancient breed from the rugged mountains of Wales is the Welsh pony, a hardy and versatile pony ranging from 40" to 58". Welsh ponies were first brought to America in the 1800's. There are two divisions of Welsh ponies, Class A ponies measuring 50" or 12.2 hands or less, and Class B ponies over 50" or 12.2 hands but not over 58" or 14.2 hands. Welsh ponies can be any color except pinto.

The Welsh pony is a very attractive pony with an aristocratic head and well-proportioned body, and is known for his courage, intelligence, and stamina. The eyes are bold and set well apart, ears small, neck slender and lengthy, the shoulders long and sloping well back, the back is muscular and strong, and the tail is carried gaily.

Welsh ponies are excellent for beginning riders as well as the more advanced. Their versatility is impressive, as they perform well under saddle for Western and English pleasure riding and equitation, hunting and jumping, harness, parades, stock horse, and endurance riding.

They are also popular for cross-breeding with horses, especially with Thoroughbreds, to produce a larger, equally versatile pony with a good nature.

Red Rocket, a Welsh pony, is a star Pony Club performer with 11-year-old Allison.

The Irish Fair gives Holly, 13, a chance to dress in costume to ride her Connemara pony, Emmy. The pony's nice conformation eliminates many causes of lameness.

Another popular pony breed in America is the Connemara. The Connemara pony's native home is the western coast of Ireland called Connaught. The Connemara's exact origin is unknown, but it is generally believed to be a cross between the native pony of that area and Spanish horses imported by horse breeders of Ireland during the years of commercial trade with Spain. The contribution of Spanish blood to the Connemara pony is quite evident.

The Connemara was first imported to the U.S. in 1951. Because of the extent of Arabian blood and their larger size, Connemaras are perhaps more in demand for "advanced beginners" and intermediate riders rather than for total beginners. Connemaras are very popular for both riding and driving. They perform well under harness and in dressage, hunting, and jumping competitions even while carrying heavy weights. They have outstanding jumping ability.

The height of Connemaras in North America ranges from 13 hands to over 15 hands. However, if a Connemara is shown in a pony class in a division other than Connemara, he must be 14.2 or under. He can be any color except pinto or cream with blue eyes.

The Connemara pony is rugged and sturdy with a well-shaped head and large, kind eyes, a neck of good length, compact body and broad chest, shoulders long and sloping, and well rounded hindquarters. The Connemara is very hardy and sure-footed, known for his stamina, adaptability, versatility, and his sensible and willing disposition.

The American Quarter Pony is a revival of the original small Quarter Horse of colonial days before so much Thoroughbred blood was in-

Teresa, 15, is mounted on her Quarter Pony, C.C., whose versatility is impressive. C.C. can do almost everything—Western classes, halter and performance, gymkhana, and English classes, including Hunter Hack.

troduced to increase his speed. The Quarter Pony stands between 11.2 and 14.2 hands, and must have Quarter Horse conformation and color, excluding Appaloosa, Albino, or Pinto characteristics.

The Quarter Pony is heavily-muscled with a deep heart girth, muscular hindquarters, and a wide chest with the forelegs set well apart. The head should be in proportion to the body, with large wide-set eyes and medium sized ears.

His disposition is kind, gentle, and even-tempered, making him an ideal horse for beginning riders. Although small, he is stocky enough to carry larger riders. He is as versatile as his ancestor, the Quarter Horse, performing well under both English and Western tack.

Several other pony breeds suitable for kids exist, but do not occur in large numbers in the United States. Among these are the Haflinger Ponies, Norwegian Fjord Ponies, Gotland Ponies, and American Walking Ponies.

If your kid has grown tall enough and is physically adept, she may be ready for a real horse.

We have already discussed the variations of individuals within a breed, and the great value of cross-breds. If you want some kind of a starting place among breeds, you will probably find the greatest number of sensible horses among Quarter Horses with little or no Thoroughbred blood in them. Another excellent choice is the Morgan horse. It follows that grade horses with a lot of Morgan or Quarter Horse blood in them can be good. Every real horseman knows of one or two horses in almost every breed that might be good for kids, but we're talking about averages, not exceptions.

Quarter Horses were probably developed in the earliest days of the American colonies when horse racing became a popular diversion. No one had TV or video but almost everyone had horses, and racing them was fun. All the horse owners needed was a thin strip of cleared land. By the time a town sprang up in the clearing, the strip was about a quarter of a mile long. What was more natural than for Main Street to become a quarter-mile racetrack?

Early Colonials discovered that the crossing of Thoroughbreds with local Indian pony stock of Spanish origin produced a horse with remarkable acceleration and speed, essential for success on the quarter-mile track. Horses bred for this kind of racing soon became known as Quarter Horses. As the pioneers went West, they took with them their Quarter Horses and their sport of racing a quarter mile. Quarter Horse racing is now one of the most popular and lucrative of Western sports.

When the cowboys adopted Quarter Horses for their mounts, they discovered the Quarter Horse's talent for working cattle. They were not only sensible, but quick at turning, starting, and stopping, and they had the hardiness necessary for survival on the Western range. Two kinds of Quarter Horses evolved, the longer-striding faster horse for racing, and the sturdy quick-thinking cow pony. This latter type often makes an excellent child's horse.

The cow pony type of Quarter Horse is compact, muscular (but not as heavily muscled as in earlier days), with sloping shoulders, big chest, sloping croup, a well-formed head, small ears, straight face, and a prominent jaw. He is a versatile horse and has a gentle, sensible nature ideal for children. For beginning riders, he can be a kind teacher and a great confidence builder.

His versatility makes him a capable performer in many English sports as well as Western. He is often seen in the dressage arena, jumping ring, and in Eventing.

Another good-natured horse for children is the first strictly American breed—the Morgan Horse. The little bay colt foaled in the late 1780's in Vermont was later named Justin Morgan after his owner. Historians disagree about the colt's lineage, but everyone agrees that his prepotency has left its stamp upon American horseflesh. The colt's progeny were so like him that they were called "Morgans." Thus the colt became the

Cross-country obstacles pose no problem for Allison, 14, and her Quarter Horse, Chico.

Wendy, seven, and David, four, enjoy riding Misty, their registered Morgan horse, because of her super good disposition.

progenitor for an entire new breed known for its remarkable disposition, versatility, strength, and "class," qualities in great demand in early America and even today.

The Morgan has a medium head and a slightly tapering muzzle, fine pointed ears, sloping shoulders and prominent withers, a rounded croup, a muscled body set squarely on well-muscled legs, and good feet. Morgans are larger now than in Colonial days, and range from 14.2 to 15.2 hands.

A show-type Morgan has been developed which shines in the show ring as a park horse or roadster (harness horse). But the older classic type of Morgan is increasingly popular and is good for young novice riders because they are usually kind, willing, and easy to handle. Morgans experience longevity, so an older Morgan who has been around can give a youngster many happy years of companionship.

Even if the horse or pony you are looking at seems just right for your kid in every way, there is one more very important factor—personality. Just as two persons can be very good people but are not able to live happily with each other, so a horse and rider may both be very good, but can't get along together. For the rider to do well, this "matching" of horse and rider is essential. If your kid does not "like" a certain horse, or feels that the horse doesn't "like" her, she's probably right. Later when she is more experienced, it won't be as crucial, but now while she is starting out, it's best to cross off that horse from your list, and look for another. Eventually you will find one.

Let us suppose that your kid and her new horse are well matched. The horse has joined your family, and the relationship looks great.

Relationships are never static. Let's see how your kid's relationship with her horse is going to change.

Chapter 19

The Rules Of The Game

A group becomes a herd....instinct for organization and social order....establishing the rules....acceptable and unacceptable behavior....learning by reward and punishment....the three R's of a good relationship.... love is the key....three ways to help your kid.

When we moved from the city to our ranch in the Sierra Nevada foothills many years ago, we were apprehensive about moving the horses. We planned to trailer them up in the late summer, when the grass would be brown, so we wouldn't have to worry about too rich a pasture. They would be out grazing during the day, and kept in the barnyard at night. We would continue to feed them alfalfa twice a day so they could adjust gradually to the change in their diet.

But all the horses had been raised as individuals in stalls, and we planned to turn them loose together to run over several hundred acres. How would they behave?

As the horses were unloaded from the trailer, they swung around at the end of their tie ropes and snorted and blew. Set free, they trotted slowly out into the fields, stopping from time to time to stare around as if they could hardly believe their eyes. It was fun watching them explore their new home. Before long they were grazing contentedly, with occasional breaks for hi-jinks—running and leaping and bounding and chasing each other.

To our amazement, in less than two weeks our motley group of horses had become a well-structured herd. The oldest gelding, a former racehorse, was the leader, and a Quarter Horse/Thoroughbred buckskin mare, always a bossy individual, was the leader's assistant, the lead mare. Each horse had his place in the social structure—a firmly-established pecking order. The old gelding obviously told the lead mare when it was time to eat, when to play, when to drink, when to sleep—and who was to stay on guard. The buckskin mare passed along the orders, and every horse obeyed. It was a happy herd.

Not one of those horses had had prior experience with liberty. Apparently their instinct for survival developed a social structure with rules which promoted the safety and welfare of the group. Even the old gelding, who was far better acquainted with racetracks than with open range, knew exactly how to organize his herd by imposing discipline.

Imposing discipline is not punishment. Right from the Random House dictionary my favorite definition of that word reads, "Discipline is instruction and exercise designed to train proper conduct." *Discipline is establishing the rules of the game,* and the game is survival.

Over and over we see demonstrated this basic instinct for organization to promote the safety and welfare of a group. Kids from an early age will form their "clicks" and private clubs, some with rituals and passwords. At the levels of higher education, sororities and fraternities fill the need for this type of organization.

Children and horses subconsciously *want* these rules, not only for their well-being, but for survival.

A year after moving the horses to the ranch, we introduced a new horse to the herd, and we watched the interplay as the established family taught the newcomer their rules. He was instructed mostly by the lead gelding and lead mare, but all the horses contributed to his education. He was allowed to graze and was given attention and nuzzling and neck-grooming—all rewards—when his behavior was acceptable. When it was not, he was ignored or nipped and kicked—punished. With consistent discipline, he quickly learned the rules. In a few weeks his place in the pecking order of the herd was established and secure.

When a relationship is between members of two different species, as between a human and a horse, establishing the rules of the game is even more important because of the difference in size and vulnerability. The horse you acquired for your kid already knows about pecking order. He must acknowledge that the one who cares for him and rides him is to be respected. His behavior must be acceptable to your kid, small as she is.

Acceptable behavior includes good ground manners—he stands still when he's being brushed, he holds his head down when the bridle is put on, he stands quietly while he is being mounted. Unacceptable behavior is the opposite—he swings around while being groomed, he throws his head up when the bridle is put on, and he moves off as the rider is mounting. A horse that is good for a kid will have been taught behavior that is acceptable.

But when something new comes up, how is your kid going to tell him what she wants—what is good and what is not?

Let me emphasize that your novice rider kid should not have a horse that needs training and a lot of correction. But new situations will arise, and it's important that your kid understand the psychology of the horse's learning process. This is important to riders of all levels.

The POA, Ukiah, appreciates being told by 11-year-old Tommy that he has done a great job.

The horse is not going to read the book. A horse learns only by association with consistent reward and punishment. He associates his own actions with his rider's reactions. "Discipline is instruction and exercise designed to train proper conduct." When he gets a pat on the neck and hears the words, "Good horse!" he knows he pleased his rider. When he gets scolded or smacked, he knows he didn't. He cannot read his rider's mind, but he understands reward and correction. Horses, like children, would much rather be praised than punished.

Some horses will practically turn themselves inside out to please their riders. I remember beginning work with a big bay horse that had just come in to our barn. He was not a bad horse but he evidently had been punished frequently. He went with his ears flat, his tail clamped, and his feet dragging, as though expecting to be beaten at any minute.

I rode him for a while and asked for some ordinary figures of circles and figure eights, and when we finished I patted him and told him he was a good horse. Immediately he perked up, ears alert, whole body poised for action. It was just as though he said, "You mean I did something right? What did I do?" That horse was a joy to work with. He used to get very excited trying to figure out exactly what I wanted so he could do it right and get patted!

When a horse is good, he should be "told" so, by the proper word or a pat. He needs to know he is pleasing his person. A rider can expect to work a horse hard during his lesson. If, at the end of the session, the rider pats him and tells him he was good, the horse will probably look forward to his next lesson, no matter how hard he worked.

Your kid must be fair, be reasonable, and be consistent. If a horse swishes his tail at a fly and the kid is in the way and gets "stung" by the tail, it is not fair to punish the horse. If a horse is tied up to a post for a long time, he will move around at the post—and it is not reasonable to punish him for moving around. When a horse does do something for which he needs correction, the rider must be consistent with correction each time. If the horse is punished only some of the time for a certain behavior, he will not be able to figure out what his rider really wants.

How does one correct or punish a horse? As a parent you know that in dealing with your kid each situation is different. Taking away a privilege is probably one of the best ways of correcting a kid's unacceptable behavior, but you can't "ground" a horse, or keep him home from an overnight at a friend's.

Most experienced riders always carry something for correction, just in case. For jumping, many prefer a bat—a short riding crop with a soft leather flap at the end that makes a loud noise but doesn't hurt much. For dressage, it is the custom to carry a dressage whip which is long and thin with a "tickler" at the end of it. Western riders can use the end of the reins. Most of the time a sharp "No!" is sufficient correction, or a single tap with the bat or whip. The punishment must fit the crime and the horse. Some horses are crushed by one vocal reprimand; others need perhaps two or three spanks with the bat or whip behind the rider's leg. The horse should *never* be hit in front of the girth—the head and neck are strictly off limits for spanking.

The most common problem a novice rider has is asking the horse to do something, but because of inexperience, not giving the right cues. Of course the horse won't obey.

Whenever your kid's horse doesn't obey her, she has to think hard—

did he really mean to disobey, or did she not give him the right command? If the instruction wasn't right, it's not fair to punish him, but she should repeat the command again, more clearly. If she is certain he was naughty on purpose, she should correct him immediately. But break the bad news to your kid: *with a novice rider, almost always it is the rider's fault.*

If your kid is certain the horse did not obey on purpose, he must be corrected *immediately*, and immediately means within three or four seconds, or it doesn't do any good. A horse's mind won't make the connection if his rider waits longer than that.

If the disobedience is bad enough for a stronger correction, such as a smack with a bat, the rider must never smack the horse more than three times. The horse will understand what he is being corrected for. But if your kid continues to hit him, on the fourth time the horse will want to know, "Now what was *that* for?" It may seem funny, but that is the way a horse's mind works.

At a horse show a long time ago I was in the crowd watching a stadium jumping round. We were distressed to see one rather nice horse being ridden very poorly. The rider was doing everything wrong when he brought the horse up to the fence, so it was no surprise when the horse refused. The rider, however, blamed the horse and beat the horse with his crop. The audience began to murmur disapproval.

At the second refusal, more beatings, and a louder noise from the crowd. At the third refusal (which eliminated the rider) the horse could no longer take the injustice of the punishment, and when the rider began to beat him again, the horse threw a fit and bucked the rider off. I've always wondered what went through the rider's mind when there arose from the audience a tremendous cheer for the horse!

Lucinda Green, the great rider of the British Combined Training Team, is beloved by her horses. We watched her ride during the Los Angeles Olympics, and we enjoy playing over again our video tapes of that ride. As her horse Regal Realm takes off over each enormous jump, Lucinda lets the reins slide completely through her fingers to give the horse freedom for his effort. The moment the horse lands and gallops on, she reaches forward and gives the horse several big pats, and *then* she gathers up the reins.

Some horses, especially those kind to kids, are simply slow to obey, and the command must be repeated several times. If your kid complains about this, urge her not to give up, but to keep on giving the command. She should engrave on her heart the following message: "When your horse finds out that *you* aren't going to give up, *he* will!"

If your kid gives up and lets the horse have his way, she has lost more than a little argument; she has lost the respect of the horse. He may ever after try to make her give up first, and soon riding will not be much fun for your kid. It's important for your kid to ask the horse for what she knows she can get, and stick to it till she gets it—or get help.

Many years ago I was riding a friend's horse up a trail, and for some reason known only to the horse, he decided he was not going through the gate on the trail. He had gone through many times, but today he decided things were different. I did not have a whip, and he was too tall for me to dismount, break off a branch to use, and remount without a great deal of difficulty. The harder I kicked the horse, the more steps he took backward. I knew I had to get him through the gate or forever expect disobedience. In my desperation I began backing him on purpose—in a big circle. I backed him all the way around and through the gate and about fifty feet on the other side of the gate stopped him and patted him and told him he was a good horse for going through the gate. He was furious at first, blowing and staring around and wondering how he had gotten through. Then he suddenly relaxed and was perfectly obedient from that time on.

Just as a horse acknowledges the leader of his herd, the horse must acknowledge his rider as his leader in their relationship. As your kid and her horse get to know each other better, their relationship will gradually change. It will either grow or deteriorate.

The best foundation for a satisfying relationship lies in the "Three R's." The "Three R's" are Respect, Responsibility, and Responsiveness. They apply to any relationship—a friendship, a marriage, or a family. Your kid can apply them to her horse. If they learn to respect each other, to be responsible for each other, and to respond to each other's feelings, they will become a strong team.

Your kid should acknowledge her horse's sense of justice and respect his limitations as well as his abilities. If she treats him fairly and doesn't ask for more than he can give, he will respect her. Your kid must be responsible for his welfare, seeing that his psychological as well as physical needs are met. In return, her horse must be responsible for obedience to your kid's commands.

Last of all, your kid should learn to be sensitive to the horse's non-verbal communication, and respond to him accordingly. When she does, he will respond to her because real communication is a two-way street. A horse trained in this way obeys willingly through love, not fear.

A horse that is taught by fear will, in time of crisis, run from his trainer because he cannot trust that person. A horse that is taught by love will, in time of crisis, turn to his person for help.

Much of what I have written here about discipline and establishing the rules of the game is something that a really good instructor will teach your kid. I've included it here because it's helpful for you as a parent to know what your kid has to cope with.

If your kid doesn't have an instructor and her only alternative is learning all by herself, you can do three things to be helpful. The obvious one of course is to be sure she has a suitable horse, one that is well trained and that will take good care of her. The second is to watch for notices of clinics given from time to time in your vicinity by well-known trainers. Make it a family affair and take your kid and go. Last of all, you can help her build a good reference library of books and tapes on horsemanship.

Reading good books can help her a great deal. A number of basic books on both English and Western riding are listed in the back. Besides books, there are now outstanding video tapes of riding instruction. If you have a home recording system, renting or borrowing the tapes will work wonders for your kid's education. Even certain of the local public libraries have video tapes on this subject. If they don't, some libraries respond to public demand. You might enlist your friends to help you lobby for some equine videos. One picture is worth a thousand words, especially in teaching horsemanship. Every horse magazine has ads for videos on riding, some of them by world class riders and trainers. A home video system can be invaluable in teaching.

From time to time kids get sick or hurt; so do horses. You know what to do about a sick kid; the next chapter will give you some help in what to do about a sick horse.

Chapter 20

Without Blue Cross Or Medicare

Description of a well horse....taking PRT....vet numbers, first aid kit, first aid instructions....the 2 emergencies—colic and profuse bleeding....the 3 observations before calling....the 5 kinds of wounds ....lameness....preventive measures....hot bran mash....nursing care.

I took my sick child to a certain pediatrician for the first time and was surprised when he asked me what was wrong with her. I protested, "But that's what you're supposed to tell *me*!" He smiled apologetically. "I mean, what makes you think she is sick?" That was a question I could answer.

Some morning your kid may go out to feed her horse, and come back to the house all upset because he's not acting the way he usually does. Just as you know right away when something is wrong with your kid because she's acting differently, so your kid will know when something is wrong with her horse.

If the horse is at a stable where *experienced* horsemen are available, she can get their advice on whether or not to call the vet. Veterinarians usually list the four real emergencies as profuse bleeding, colic, eye injuries, and foaling. The people at the stables ought to be able to classify the problem, call the vet if necessary, and help your kid and her horse.

Your kid will know right away then there's something wrong with her horse, especially if he looks like any of these. Clockwise from left—strangles, laminitis, and colic.

If the horse is in your backyard or a neighbor's, your kid may beg you to come and look at him, even though she knows you don't know anything about horses. Most people can look at other people's sick or injured horses and be calm about it, but an owner often comes unglued.

To know when a horse is in trouble, a person has to know what a horse in good health looks and acts like. Long before anything goes wrong, you and your kid should study her healthy horse. Here's what you should see:

His ears will be pricked and moving, and he will look alert and interested with eyes bright and shining and looking for something to eat. His tongue, inside his lips, and the lining of his nostrils will be pink.

His coat will be short and glossy with the hair lying flat. In winter it may be thick and shaggy, but it will be sleek and lying flat just the same.

His skin will be loose and easily moved over the bones when your kid lays her hand flat on it and presses while making a circle with her hand.

His body will be well filled out but not swollen. If your kid puts her ear against one of his flanks, she will hear all kinds of rumbling and gurgling going on.

He will be standing squarely on all four legs. A horse may rest one hind foot by cocking it, but never a fore foot. When he is taken out of his stall or paddock and walked up and down, his weight is distributed evenly on all four legs. When he is "jogged out," he will take strides of equal length and his head will not nod or bob.

He will be eager to eat, and he will clean up his food.

His urine can range from clear to cloudy, from no color to amber color, and it will be passed several times a day.

His droppings will be in damp balls with no bad odor, and their color will depend on his diet. Alfalfa gives bright green manure when just passed, and oat hay or dried pasture grass gives brown manure. It will not be loose and there will be around eight piles every 24 hours.

His pulse, respiration rate, and temperature, known as PRT, will be normal. You'll recall writing down the horse's PRT at the vet check to record them later on his I.D. card posted by his halter. It's a good idea to practice taking the horse's PRT while he is feeling good so you won't be so nervous if you have to take it when he's sick.

Taking the pulse and respiration rate is easier if there are two of you. Your kid can tie the horse to the tie rail. One person (your kid) can find the pulse or breathing and do the counting, and the other (you) can watch the second hand of a wrist watch. A horse doesn't stand still for long, so it's customary to count for only 15 seconds and multiply by four. Repeat this several times to be sure.

His pulse will be from 36 to 42 beats per minute. It has to be counted with fingertips and never a thumb—which would give the pulse of the human. It is interesting to note that it is quite normal for a horse to actually skip heart beats, such as 1 every 6 or 8 beats. An athletic horse has a lower heart rate, perhaps 28 to 30, and his heart skips quite a few beats.

Unfortunately a horse's pulse is usually hard to find. Places where you and your kid might be able to find his pulse are:

1. underneath and inside the big jaw bone where you can press the big artery against the bone,

2. in the little hollow on either side of the base of the neck where it joins his chest,

3. the artery on the horse's cheek, just above and behind the eye, and

4. on the inside (not the back) of the foreleg, level with the knee-joint, where an artery passes over the bone.

You may have to take it several times to be sure.

His respiration rate will be from 8 to 12 inhalations per minute. It's so long between breaths that you could even think he's stopped breathing. If he's quiet and relaxed, you can count each time the rims of his nostrils go in and out. It might be easier to count each time his flanks go out and in. His flank movement can best be seen while standing almost behind the horse. Since he may take a breath only every seven or eight seconds, your kid will have to be patient and observant.

An inexperienced person shouldn't try to take the horse's temperature, but your kid may be able to find a knowledgeable person willing to help. You should have on hand an equine thermometer, and the mercury should be shaken down to low before using it. An equine thermometer is molded with a loop at the top end of it, through which you should tie a string at least 12" long, and then make a loop in the end of the string.

The string loop is to be slipped over one finger of the person taking the horse's rectal temperature, or the string can be tied onto a clothes pin and the clothes pin clipped to the horse's tail. This will prevent breakage if the thermometer is "pooped out" unexpectedly. If the thermometer should be pulled up into the horse's rectum, the person can pull it back out with the string. If your kid says, "How gross!," remember I never did say taking care of a horse was easy.

A horse's normal rectal temperature will range from 99 to 101 degrees.

It is higher in the afternoon than in the morning, much higher after exercise, and also higher on a hot day than a cold one. A horse with 101 degree temperature in the early morning probably has a fever.

You might be interested in knowing how much your horse weighs—without taking him to a truck scales. (1) You measure the heart girth in inches—the line completely around the horse just back of his front legs. (2) You measure the length of his body in inches from the point of his shoulder to the point of his buttock. (See the chart on Parts of the Horse.)

(3) You multiply heart girth x hearth girth x length, divide this figure by 300, add 50, and you have the weight of the horse within 3% of his weight on scales.

Before the horse is brought to his new home, you should decide on the veterinarian you will call for advice and for emergencies. In fact, you should have the names and numbers of two or three vets in case the one you want isn't available. Post their phone numbers clearly by the telephone along with the other emergency numbers you keep.

You already have a first-aid kit at home for your family members. Now you should prepare a first-aid kit for the horse, to be kept in the barn preferably in a closed cabinet where supplies can be kept clean and horses and small children cannot get to it. Bandages and dressings can be put in plastic bags.

Before a vet is needed, talk to the vet who is your first choice. Ask him what medications and supplies he would suggest you have on hand in addition to what's on the list.

The variety of items will depend on your location, as country calls can be quite different from calls to suburban stables. Horses in different parts of the country are subject to different types of ailments. To complete your list, buy what you need from the vet's office, a vet supply store, or vet catalog, rather than a drug store. Having everything on hand for emergencies pays off.

In addition to the first-aid supplies, have handy in the cabinet a book or relevant pages photocopied from a book, enclosed in plastic protectors, giving you guidelines and procedures for handling emergencies so you don't have to run back to the house, look for the book, and thumb through a lengthy index. Always call the vet in emergencies, but there are two cases in which you have to act immediately.

The two most urgent cases are (1) colic, and (2) an injury with profuse bleeding.

Colic doesn't take long to diagnose. A horse with colic is suffering from stomach pain, and the pain scares him. He keeps looking around at his stomach, and he may be trying to bite it or kick it. He often keeps lying down and getting up again, or rolls, paws, and even throws himself on the ground.

Suggested First Aid Supplies for Horses

(Check this list with your vet)

small plastic bucket reserved for vet use only

thermometer (preferably equine type with loop)

scissors (preferably curved)

1 pr. rubber or plastic surgical gloves

clean towels

1 20 cc. syringe

2 18 gauge x 1½ needles

large bottle of disinfectant (recommended by your vet)

soft scrub brush

antiseptic soap

antibiotic powder (preferred by your vet)

antibiotic salve or cream (preferred by your vet)

colic medicine (recommended by your vet)

oral anti-inflammatory drug (recommended by your vet)

hydrogen peroxide

liniment (preferred by your vet)

antibiotic ophthalmic ointment—NO STEROIDS (recommended by your vet)

salts (Epsom type) for soaking

6 sterile gauze pads, at least 3" or 4" square

2 rolls of gauze, 6" wide

2 rolls 4" wide cotton bandages

1 roll of sterile cotton (1 pound)

1 roll of sheet cotton for bandages (tack shop)

1 government surplus 22' x 18" field bandage (very useful)

4"wide eight-foot long flannel bandages (make your own)

2 rolls 4" wide tape bandages—cling-type

large safety pins

adhesive tape

masking tape

rubbing alcohol

boric acid powder

petroleum jelly

It's important that you or your kid immediately put a halter on the horse, get him up if he is down, and start walking him to keep him from throwing himself down and hurting himself. Don't give the horse any kind of medication until you talk to the vet—and send someone else to call him while you keep the horse walking unless your kid can handle the horse by herself.

The other immediate emergency is profuse bleeding from a wound. Don't put medication of any kind on the wound. Try to stop the bleeding. Usually a pressure bandage will do it—a bunch of gauze squares or a small towel or wad of cotton—pressed over the wound and then wrapped firmly with a roll of track bandage. If a major artery or vein is cut you may have to apply a pressure bandage above the wound also, or in extreme cases, apply a tourniquet above the wound. The tourniquet must be loosened every 20 minutes. Have someone else call the vet while you stay with the horse.

In cases not so urgent, you and your kid will have time to make certain observations before you phone the vet. Accuracy in reporting will make it easier for him to judge how much of an emergency exists.

Three things are important to describe to the vet when you call: the horse's *appetite*, his *attitude*, and his present *activity* or symptoms. To paraphrase my pediatrician, "What is the horse doing that makes you think he is sick?"

Appetite helps diagnose illness. If the horse isn't eating, he is really sick. Horses enjoy eating, and are used to grazing more or less around the clock. A refusal to eat is a symptom that the vet needs to know about.

The horse's attitude is important. Attitude means whether he is lively, quiet, nervous, restless, depressed, violent, or whatever. The vet will want to know what is different from his usual attitude.

Last of all, his present activity—what the horse is doing that's different. If he usually just stands and now he's restless and walking, this gives the vet a clue. And vice versa. If your kid can say, "Well, he won't eat and he's standing in a corner with his head down and he's coughing a lot and his nose is running," it's more helpful than just saying he's sick. If the horse normally doesn't take a nap until noon but this morning he's lying on his back close to a fence with his legs up in the air and he won't get up, the vet will tell you what to do until he gets there.

In case of illness, the PRT is helpful, but if you and your kid can't take the horse's PRT, don't worry about it. Note what the horse's breathing is like. Is it faster than normal? Look at the color inside his nostrils. Have your kid flip up his upper lip so you can see the color of his lips and gums. If, instead of normal bright pink, they are white or blue or very dark colored, the vet needs to know right away.

Other symptoms of illness to note are sweating, shivering, the coat staring (not lying flat and glossy), eyes dull and ears drooping, no sounds in his belly, lack of evidence of urination or defecation, and anything else that differs from the well horse.

If you know what may have caused the problem, such as excessive exercise or a sick horse next door or leaving open the feed room door, be sure to tell the vet. Most important of all—follow his instructions.

Prevention of accidents is easier than treating them, and removing objects on which horses can hurt themselves will save you and your kid a lot of grief—and money. But in spite of all precautions, horses, like children, fool around a lot and do get hurt. Some people say a horse is an accident looking for a place to happen.

This is not a first aid manual, but if you and your kid know the different classes of injuries a horse can suffer, you'll have a better idea of how fast to call the vet. He'll know best what to do. You don't take your kid to the doctor every time she skins her knees, and having the vet come out isn't always necessary. Many of the minor wounds will get well with just some first aid, but an injured horse needs care more promptly than cats or dogs or other domestic animals. Phone your vet and take his advice.

The five kinds of wounds are bruises, abrasions, incisions, lacerations, and punctures.

A bruise, such as from a kick or a blow or a fall, does not break the skin but causes swelling and tenderness and, when located in certain places, lameness. The swelling comes from internal bleeding caused by the blow.

A larger bruise may result in a blood blister beneath the skin called a hematoma which still may not be visible to a person. Old horsemen know of an interesting way of learning just where the blow actually occurred. The horse is tied up in the sun so that the injured side is exposed to the warm sun. Real soapflakes (shaved Ivory or Castile soap, NOT a detergent) are put in a bowl and beaten hard with just enough hot water to make a mixture the consistency of whipped cream. This mixture is then spread all over the general area where the hematoma is suspected, and allowed to dry in the sun. In an hour or so the soap will have dried up and practically disappeared, *except over the bruise*. The heat of the injury will prolong the life of the soapsuds and will outline almost the exact print of the blow.

An abrasion is an area where the skin has been scraped off, like a floor-burn acquired in basketball. Horses usually get it as a rope burn or from improperly fitted tack rubbing the skin till it opens. The wound is raw, painful, and will ooze clear fluid or blood.

An incision is a clean cut by something sharp such as a piece of glass or the edge of a piece of metal. The biggest danger is from excessive bleeding.

A laceration is a tearing of the skin or flesh by a projection such as a nail or sharp end of a branch.

A puncture wound is usually caused by stepping on a nail or by a splinter, and may be deep even though the surface area injured is small. It is serious because of the danger that the wound may close over on the outside, sealing in bacteria which cause infection.

The four stages in treatment are stopping the bleeding, cleaning the wound, dressing it, and protecting it if necessary. Each type of wound requires a different treatment, and your vet will know the best course to follow. Some wounds are better left unbandaged to heal in the open air. You might reassure your kid—often the most awful-looking wounds heal quickly and leave little or no scar tissue.

If the horse is lame, describe the symptoms—slightly off when jogged out, or won't bear weight at all, or a toe is rested, or pointed, if there is swelling, heat, or if he tries to put most of his weight on the hind legs, etc.

You might not know if a horse is lame unless you are aware of his three gaits when he is sound. At the walk, he moves one hindleg first, then the foreleg on the same side, then the other hindleg, and the other foreleg. There are four distinct hoof beats in even succession, so the walk is called a four-beat lateral gait. The trot or jog is a two-beat diagonal gait, that is, he moves the diagonal pairs of legs in unison. The canter is a three-beat gait in which he strikes off with one hindleg, then moves the other hindleg in unison with its diagonal foreleg, and last the other foreleg. This is followed by a moment of suspension when all four legs are off the ground.

Lameness with no sign of injury may be difficult to diagnose. After your kid is more experienced in riding, she may be the first to notice the lameness while she is riding, even at the walk, because the horse will feel "off." If she can count the footfalls at the walk she may be able to notice if there is a pause in the rhythm between any two of the steps. The lame leg usually is the one that follows a pause because the horse is reluctant to put it down, and it's followed by a quick step.

She should dismount in any event, and "jog out" the horse while someone else (you?) watches his head to see if the head is nodding or bobbing instead of staying steady. His head is a counterbalance, and he uses it to take the weight off the hurt foot whenever it touches the ground.

Before you call the vet, you or your kid can feel up and down the leg to see if there is anything unusual in the lame leg—and feeling both front or both hind legs at the same time is the best way to tell. Sometimes a new lump shows up, and sometimes you can even feel heat in one leg and not in the other. Be as observant as you can in the way the horse looks and moves, and report it to the vet.

The state of health of a horse is like that of your kid—and everyone else in your family. Prevention of illness or injury is far easier than a cure.

Perhaps the most important way to prevent illness lies in following the ten rules of good feeding in Chapter 11. I suggest that your kid copy them and post them in the barn. If your kid follows those rules, her horse will be much less likely to develop digestive problems.

The second most important preventive measure is regular worming and innoculations. All horses have internal parasites, and if they are not dealt with on a regular basis they can cause serious and permanent internal damage. The parasites most commonly present in a horse are large and small strongyles, round worms or ascarids, pinworms, and the larvae of the botfly. Each causes damage in its own way, from burrowing into and eating the lining of the intestines, to burrowing into the walls of the small arteries, causing inflammation and blood clots or rupture of the arteries. Since parasites hatch, grow, and reproduce on a regular cycle, they can be controlled *only by a regular treatment program*. Keeping clean the area of the horse's barn or paddock is also a necessary deterrent to parasite infestation.

The two most common ways of worming a horse are by "tubing" and by "pasting." Until recently, tubing was the only method. The veterinarian passes a long plastic tube into the horse's stomach through the horse's nose, and then puts the worm-killer into the tube from a plastic squeeze bottle and makes sure it all goes down into the horse.

The pasting method involves a big plastic syringe containing the worm medicine in a paste. The tip of the syringe is inserted at the side of the horse's mouth back between the molars and the cheek, and then the medicine is pushed into the mouth with the plunger of the syringe.

Over the past few years great progress has been made in developing effective wormers, but at the same time some parasites are developing immunity to certain wormers. Your geographical location has a lot to do with the time of year and type of worming for your kid's horse. It's best for you and your kid to talk to your veterinarian and establish a regular schedule for worming. The better the vet knows your kid and her horse, the more helpful he can be.

One quick word about the vet's visit. Occasionally a horse is resistant to being treated, and the vet uses a "twitch" to keep him quiet during the treatment. This usually consists of a metal device that is fastened around the horse's upper lip to squeeze it. The horse immediately stands still. Your kid will feel a whole lot better if she understands that it is *not pain* that causes him to stand still but something called endorphins released by the brain into the horse's bloodstream upon squeezing the sensitive lip. Endorphins are like opiates that raise the horse's pain threshold so he actually feels much less pain and becomes more relaxed.

Regular innoculations against the most deadly and common diseases are a must. A yearly tetanus shot can prevent the dread disease of lockjaw; the fatal disease of sleeping sickness fortunately now has a vaccine; the common, debilitating, and sometimes fatal flu can be prevented by innoculations, as can Potomac fever. The innoculations necessary also depend upon your geographical location and time of year. With your veterinarian, set up a regular schedule—and stick to it!

At the time of the vet's visit, always have him check the horse's teeth. A horse's teeth keep growing all his life. The horse chews from side to side, on one side of his jaw at a time, so that his chewing is supposed to wear down the growing molars to a smooth surface. If something happens to prevent some of the molars from being worn down, the resulting sharp points can cut the horse's cheeks or tongue and make chewing very painful. Sometimes food will fall unchewed out of his mouth, or the horse will stop eating. When this happens, the vet "floats" the teeth by filing down the sharp points with a big file, so the cheeks pass over the teeth without injury.

Having worming and shots and teeth checked at the same visit is not only economical for you but helps ensure the horse's health. You'll find some excellent books listed at the back which will give you more information on the health care of horses.

There is one other preventive measure available for the day your kid has had a long, hard ride or a grueling day at a gymkhana or horse show. It's giving her horse a hot bran mash in the evening before bedtime. The mash is also called a "hunter's supper" because fox hunters usually fix it for their hunting horses after an exciting day following the hounds. It's a great way to help prevent a horse having an upset stomach after a lot of excitement and changes in his feed and exercise schedules.

Your kid can take a big plastic feed bucket and put in it several quarts of wheat bran (from the feed store). Then have her add very hot water, stirring carefully, until the bran is the consistency of oatmeal. It will absorb an incredible amount of water. Then she can add some sliced carrots, a tablespoon of salt, and a handful or two of grain. Mix well, then cover the mixture with a rug or a saddle pad and let it steam until cool enough for the horse to eat. Remove the rug, stir again, and serve. Horses love it. If you think your dog is glad to see you when you come home, try carrying the bucket of bran mash down to the barn some time to your kid's horse.

A hot bran mash can be given once a week, especially in the evening after a day of strenuous work and before the day of rest. A bran mash is particularly good for sick and recuperating horses.

One other important point should be remembered about nursing a horse through an injury or an illness. The horse can't understand the words that you and the vet are saying, and he doesn't know what's wrong. He will depend entirely upon the love and kindness of his persons, and *the tone of voice of the humans with him* to know whether or not he's going to get better. A horse who is given loving care and hears cheerful and encouraging words, especially in the midst of pain, seems to have more recuperative powers than one who does not.

With almost any hobby or sport, expenses seem to mount up as the person becomes more involved. Let's talk about where to and where not to—economize.

Chapter 21

Four Feet On The Ground

*Don't compromise quality for feed, farrier, and first aid
. . . .you can economize with vet clinics. . . . fitting and
taking care of tack properly. . . .riding clinics, local
horse shows, do-it-yourself sports. . . .leave trailering to
experts. . . .definition of stable personnel.*

As horsekeeping expenses mount up, you will find ways of economizing, but the three things in which you should *never* reduce quality in order to save money are:

1. **Feed.** Always buy the best feed you can find, but shop around. Some feed stores carry the same quality for less money.

2. **Farrier** (the horseshoer). Secure as good and reliable a horseshoer as you can. Let him know that you recognize his value to your horse's welfare.

3. **First aid.** Don't put off calling the vet to save money. Sometimes five minutes on the telephone with the vet will give you the help you need without his having to come to the barn. But some people always spend too little and too late, never realizing how many good horses they have lost that could have been saved.

In rural areas, a good way to economize on vet calls is to organize an equine clinic twice a year, spring and fall, when all horses should be tube wormed and given their regular shots. When thirty or forty horses are signed up, the charge for the "barn call" is minimal. The vet goes from one place to another but he doesn't have to travel far between calls. Clients who are new in a rural area can tie a dish towel around the gate to signify they want the vet. He picks up the towel and goes in to find out what horses need to be treated.

Earlier we discussed the importance of your kid's clothing when she rides. Her horse needs clothing, too, called "tack."

Good tack is expensive. Economizing on tack may seem to be a good idea, but poor leather is a poor investment. Leather goods from Third World countries, India in particular, are poorly tanned and then dyed a rich brown so that the color comes off on sweaty palms, and the tack itself has a tendency to simply tear or break without much effort. This can lead to bloodshed.

Well-tanned American leather is now sold to Japan where it is manufactured into bridles and then brought back into the U.S. In these cases the leather is of good quality, and if you shop carefully you can acquire good tack at a reasonable cost. Leather goods made in England, Germany, and the U.S. are still the finest quality. Buying good tack and taking care of it is most economical in the long run.

You have learned how important comfort is to your kid while riding. Think how her horse must feel—he's doing all the work. His saddle and bridle must be fitted properly. Get expert help somewhere when you purchase tack for the horse, especially the saddle and bridle.

A saddle is meant to compensate for the difference between the rider's bottom and the horse's top, and to distribute the rider's weight over a larger area. The saddle must not press on the withers or the backbone of the horse. When the rider is mounted, the rider should be able to put her hand between the horse's withers and the saddle.

A quick check of the horse himself will show if the tack is rubbing him where it shouldn't. When the saddle is removed from the horse's back after exercise, there should be a dry streak over his withers and down his backbone, showing there was no pressure from the saddle. If the withers and backbone are wet all over, the horse needs a different saddle or saddle pad. The horse will have a hard time concentrating and responding to his rider when he is uncomfortable, not to mention the possibility of developing saddle sores.

Saddles are made with different sizes "trees," that is, the frame on which the saddle is built. A horse with a narrow back, high withers, and slender frame will need a saddle with a narrow tree. A horse with big broad shoulders, broad back, and broad withers, will need a saddle with a wide tree. Since most Western horses are Quarter Horses, most Western saddles are built with trees to fit a Quarter Horse, but the dry line on the horse's back is still a good test.

In English saddles there is an overwhelming choice of styles and designs. A horse with high withers must be fitted carefully to prevent pressure on his prominent bones. A cutback saddle, where the pommel is cut back instead of going straight across, doesn't always fit such a horse. Your kid riding English must have expert help in choosing a saddle.

Whatever the type of tack that your kid uses, it must be kept clean so it will last longer and be more comfortable for her and the horse. It's hard for a rider to find time to clean tack in addition to cleaning the horse and riding him, but it is an investment in the rider's safety as well as maintaining your investment in the tack itself.

Leather not properly cared for becomes dry and cracked and brittle, an accident waiting to happen. Keeping leather tack in good condition isn't difficult if your kid learns the proper treatment of leather.

I'm sure you don't put hand lotion on dirty hands—you first wash your hands. The same principle applies to leather tack. *Before any oil or conditioner is put on the tack, the dirt and sweat must first be washed off.* This is best done with warm water and real soap, like Ivory or Castile, and a dampened wrung-out sponge. Do *not* use saddle soap, which isn't a soap at all because it does not have the ingredients for lifting dirt. Saddle soap is a thick creamy substance for replacing the oils in tanned leather. If saddle soap or any other conditioner is put on dirty leather, it will carry the dirt into the leather and make a permanent stain.

Don't let your kid try to scrape off the dirt as this destroys the leather finish. If the tack is extremely dirty, she can use a mild dish-washing detergent and a soft scrub brush, like a nail brush or surgical scrub brush from hospital supply. Horse hair makes an excellent scrub brush—tie a bunch of the horse's mane or tail hairs into a knot, and re-knot it several times.

After the leather is clean and dried with a soft cloth or chamois, then your kid can apply a leather preservative such as bar glycerine (often mistakenly called saddle soap), liquid glycerine, saddle soap, or Murphys Oil Soap. These are oils and will be absorbed by the leather to keep it supple. Every couple of months she can apply a leather conditioner such as Lexol, Hydrophane, or Neatsfoot oil, but only on clean tack.

When cleaning tack, special attention should be paid to the areas receiving the greatest wear. On both Western and English bridles, the most frequent breaking points are where the reins and headstalls are attached to the bit. Somtimes one good jerk on the reins will result in disaster.

On an English saddle, the most frequent breaking point is on the stirrup leather—the stitching of the leather at the buckle where it hangs from the saddle. If a stitch or two is loose or broken, don't let your kid use that stirrup leather until you've taken it to the local leather repair shop. There are few things more unpleasant than having your kid put her weight in her heels, only to have one heel keep on going down under the horse's belly. When she is an accomplished rider, losing a stirrup isn't going to bother her at all, but by the time she is a good rider she will be taking good care of her tack without reminders from you.

Cleaning tack doesn't have to be a chore; it can be a social hour. Maybe once a month your kid would like to invite her friends over for a tack cleaning session and make it a picnic or a party. Encourage her to establish a routine for all the activities related to her horse. It will help keep her horse happy, and make her happy too.

Riding lessons are expensive, but are still the best investment you can make for your kid. If riding lessons, a Pony Club, or 4-H, are unavailable where you live, try to take her to trainers' clinics held in your area from time to time. Articles and ads in national magazines will tell you when these are held; ask to be put on the mailing list.

Katie is competing in a 50-mile Endurance Ride on her Welsh pony, Spunky, where they finished 48 out of 83 and Spunky was the smallest animal competing.

Many riders have trainers get their horses ready for shows, but there are other less expensive programs. Endurance riding and ride-and-tie events are challenging sports open to every kind of horse and most riders do not have trainers. In do-it-yourself sports such as dressage and Eventing, the rider does not turn her horse over to a trainer, but has a ground man or instructor teach her while she rides. In almost every sport there is a wide selection of instruction books and video tapes, excellent clinics, and lots of enthusiastic participants to help your kid.

The well-trained 14-year-old purebred Shetland pony, Moonlight, gives ten-year-old Julie a happy and safe ride.

Horse showing at local barn shows is an inexpensive way for your kid to start competing. Local gymkhanas are always fun, especially if they are well-organized with speed events alternating with slow ones. Local means your kid can ride her horse to and from the show and not need trailering.

Trailering a horse can range from a simple exercise to a major traumatic experience. Putting a horse into a trailer is asking him to go against all of his instincts of self-preservation. If the horse must be trailered, I suggest you get an experienced friend with a proper hauling vehicle, proper hitch, and good trailer who will help you out. If no friends are available to "share a slot" in their trailer for your horse, get professional help. The horse can tell very quickly if you don't know what you're doing. It takes a horse about two minutes to get into a bad habit, and sometimes two years to cure him of it. Until you feel very comfortable with horses and have helped a number of times in loading, hauling, and unloading horses, leave trailering your horse to the experts.

An inexpensive and one of the best ways for your kid to gain experience in caring for horses is to be a groom for an experienced rider at a large horse show or an event of some kind. No, a groom is not the lowly person of Victorian novels. She is the person responsible for the welfare of the horse, and as such is accorded great respect. Without a good groom, a rider in the higher levels of competition will not be able to concentrate fully on the job at hand.

Some years ago a column was published in the Midwest Dressage Association Journal, and with their kind permission I reprint it here.

How To Tell Stable Personnel Apart

by Ober-Rittmeister Hofrat Klausius von Turnip

The *Grand Prix Trainer* leaps indoor arenas with a single bound, is more powerful than a locomotive, faster than a speeding bullet, walks on water and gives policy to God.

The *Chief Instructor* leaps stables with a single bound, is more powerful than a switch engine, as fast as a speeding bullet, walks on water if it is calm, and talks to God.

The *Stable Manager* leaps horse vans with a running start and a good tailwind, is almost as powerful as a switch engine, faster than a speeding BB, walks on water in swimming pools and talks to God with special permission.

The *Assistant Instructor* barely clears run-in sheds, loses tugs-of-war with locomotives, can fire a speeding bullet, swims well, and is occasionally addressed by God.

The *Assistant Stable Manager* makes marks on walls attempting to leap hay barns, is run over by locomotives, can sometimes handle firearms without self-inflicted injury, treads water, and talks to animals.

The *Beginning Instructor* climbs the walls frequently, rides the rails, plays Russian Roulette, walks on thin ice, and prays a lot.

The *Working Student* runs into indoor arenas, recognizes locomotives two out of three times, is not issued ammo, can stay afloat with a life jacket, and talks to walls.

The *Beginner Student* falls over manure piles, says "look at choo-choo," wets self with water pistol, plays in mud puddles, and mumbles to self.

The *Groom* lifts indoor arenas and walks under, kicks locomotives off tracks, catches speeding bullets between his teeth, freezes water with a single glance, and IS God.

Being a groom is a position of enormous responsibility, exciting, and demanding. It's also a wonderful learning experience. If your kid gets the chance to groom for someone special at a competition, by all means, let her go for it!

Chapter 22

Eyes On The Horizon

Importance of parent power. . . . the right kind of help . . . . parents being taken advantage of. . . . the value of an object. . . . never forget to have fun. . . . success and excellence are not the same. . . . few can have success, but excellence is open to all. . . . persistence and determination are omnipotent. . . . Pegasus is a symbol.

Some years ago I was intrigued by the story of a correspondence school which began as the result of a whooping cough epidemic at the turn of the century. The outbreak temporarily played havoc with school attendance. While other school faculties suffered in silence, the dynamic young Headmaster of the Calvert School in Baltimore, Maryland, was inspired with the idea of teaching the sick children at home. The Headmaster devised a series of lessons sufficiently "fool-proof" to be taught at home by parents with no experience in teaching. When the epidemic was over, it was discovered that in many cases the students receiving instruction at home while ill were actually ahead of those who had stayed in school. The difference lay in the one-on-one instruction and the carefully crafted home lessons. The success of the home lessons launched the correspondence school.

I have since been told that the whooping cough story may be legend, that the Headmaster was simply motivated to extend education beyond the day school. Legend or not, from the six children who enrolled in the first correspondence courses in 1906, the Calvert School Home Instruction Course, covering kindergarten through eighth grade, now

Parent Power gone wrong—these poor parents should be letting their kids do the work.

has an international reputation and some 6,000 enrollments around the world every year. Calvert School students, with their parents as teachers, are known for their outstanding achievements.

This shows the power of parents when they have the right kind of guidance in helping their children.

Parent power is important when a horse becomes a member of the family, but it's equally important that the parents have some guidance in helping the kid. The wrong kind of help can turn out to be a handicap.

As a family gets more involved with the kid and her horse, the temptation grows for parents to "help" their kid more and more. Some parents start doing the things the kid ought to be doing. Before long it is the parents and not the kid who is making the effort.

The U.S. Pony Club program believes in "Parent Power" and encourages parents to be a support group, but encourages the children to manage as much as possible by themselves.

In Pony Club competitions called Rallies, the children are organized in teams with an older youngster as the stable manager. This teaches the value of teamwork as well as self-reliance. The parents are allowed to help the youngsters unload the horses and the tack trunks—and then the parents must leave the stable area or their kids will get black marks for unauthorized assistance. Parents can be supportive without being pushy.

This develops a far better attitude than the parents who are so eager for a kid to succeed that they push the youngster as though she were a pawn in an adult game. Often a kid is pushed to the extent that she is no longer comfortable nor having fun with her riding, and then the parents wonder why she wants to give it up when she was doing so well.

The opposite can be true. Sometimes a kid gets so uptight getting ready for a horse show that without realizing it she orders her parents around. She'll command them, "Bring me this!", and "Bring me that!". If a kid doesn't practice consideration of her own parents, how can she be considerate of others—and her horse? You can explain to her you've had enough and she's on her own. Then walk away. If she recovers from the shock and changes her ways, you'll have helped her more than she realizes.

You can help your kid in other ways, too.

Most of childhood's favorite fairy tales, legends, and stories have the same classic theme—the hero must conquer certain obstacles to reach a goal. He has to prove himself worthy of the prize through his own efforts.

This is not fantasy but the poetic expression of a fact of life. The hero who has to climb mountains, swim oceans, and walk through fire, is the one who gains maturity and wins his heart's desire. Sometimes giving your kid what she wants is not as valuable as giving her the opportunity to work for it. The value of an object is determined by the price you have to pay for it.

If your family is considering getting a horse for your kid, these are things to think about. Perhaps you will want to sit down with your kid and talk about what your youngster would be willing to do to earn at least part of that prize. It doesn't have to be a great deal, but you're establishing the principle. Feeding and caring for the horse comes as part of ownership; that doesn't count for earning the horse in the first place.

If your kid is quite young, there are household tasks and errands to help parents and other members of the family. You can make a wage-scale chart and post it on the wall. If she is old enough, babysitting, feeding neighbors' pets, working at other people's barns, or a part-time job in a fast food store. Suppose she howls and says her friends got horses and they didn't have to work for them. It will be interesting to see how many of those friends will lose interest in their horses within a year. The kids I know who worked in order to pay for part of the cost of their horses are more mature, dependable, and responsible for their age than their friends who did not work.

We have often heard the phrase, "Winning isn't everything; it's the only thing."

I don't agree, and I'm not alone.

Competition is an American tradition, but your kid should never let it keep her from having fun with her horse. I remember standing near the finish flags at a Horse Trials for the cross-country jumping phase when a child came galloping through the flags on her little pony. Now this pony had had three refusals at the third fence on the course and so was no longer in competition. The child was told she was eliminated, but for the purpose of schooling her pony, she could continue and finish the course.

She circled her pony, hopped off, ran up her stirrups, loosened the girth, and as she led her pony past, she looked up at me with shining eyes and glowing face. "I've never had so much fun in my whole life!" she exclaimed, and I didn't doubt it.

Don't misunderstand me—it is good to win. The athletes on the platform at the Olympics where the gold medals are awarded find it difficult to describe their feelings when they hear their own national anthem being played because they pushed themselves to the limit and won. They have surely earned all the tributes given them.

Only a handful of competitors can achieve that pinnacle of success, but there is another goal that is within the reach of every one of our kids. That goal is a standard of excellence. Excellence means the very best that a kid can do—and when she's inspired, a little bit more.

Success and excellence are not the same.

Thomas Boswell, a sportswriter for the Washington Post, wrote a column about the difference between the two. He pointed out that success often depends upon others. It is "tricky, perishable, and often outside our control." Success always brings pressure for repeated successes. This pressure can be destructive, especially when someone else achieves your goal.

On the other hand, excellence is "dependable, lasting, and largely an issue within our own control." The person who is dedicated to excellence is inspired when he sees it in others. Since he respects this quality, he can cope with being surpassed.

In horse showing, the difference between success and standards of excellence is clear. Winning a class depends not just on the performance of horse and rider, but on who the other competitors are, and who the judge is.

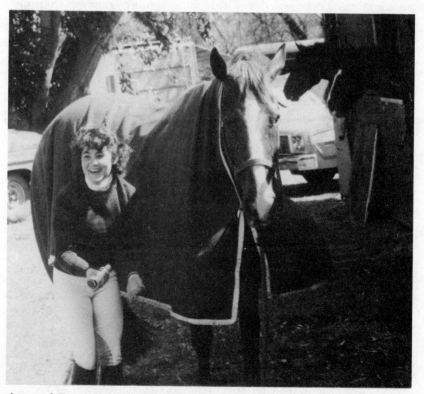

Amy and Dynamo had such a great cross-country ride that she is still in a glow, with or without ribbons.

When your kid rides her horse in the arena to the best of her ability and gets that horse to perform better than he ever has before, she has achieved as much or more than the kids with the ribbons. She may never win any ribbons at all, but with standards of excellence established in her own mind, she will develop pride in her performance and self-confidence in her ability. These are more valuable in life than physical trophies.

If your kid sometimes gets discouraged in her struggle for whatever goal she is seeking, let her consider the following.

In 1984, every member of the San Diego Padres baseball team wore on the left sleeves of their uniforms the initials R.A.K. When bystanders asked what the letters were for, they were told it was in tribute to Ray Arthur Kroc, their owner for ten years who had just died. Mr. Kroc evidently was an inspiring leader for the team. I can believe it. Many years ago I read of an interview with him in which his words inspired me as well.

Mr. Kroc declared that nothing in the world can take the place of perseverance. Talent will not, for nothing is more common than unsuccessful men with talent. Genius will not, for unrewarded genius is almost a proverb. Education will not—the world is full of educated derelicts.

"Persistence and determination alone," he concluded, "are omnipotent."

If you decide, after all this, that a horse should indeed belong in your family, I must point out to you again that a household with a horse is not a tranquil one. Your family and especially your kid will experience anguish, joy, tears, exhilaration, anxiety, happiness, worry, laughter, and pain. But in the end I do not think you will be sorry. You will have opened for your kid the door to a whole new world.

The winged horse Pegasus is not so much a myth as he is a symbol. A real horse can truly give wings to the human spirit.

Glossary of Horse Terms

action—the way the horse's feet and legs move

aids—the voice, weight, legs, and hands used in directing a horse

barrel racing—a timed event in rodeo combining speed and agility in a pattern around three barrels

blemish—an abnormality not affecting the soundness of a horse

bowed tendon—a tendon located behind the cannon bone that has become enlarged because of a severe strain

broke—tamed and trained to a certain level

buck-kneed—stands with knees too far forward

calf-kneed—stands with knees too far back

canter—an English controlled three-beat combination gait with much suspension following the third beat

capped elbow—a soft swelling at the point of the elbow

capped hock—an enlargement at the point of the hock

cinch—the strap that holds a Western saddle in place

cob—a very sturdy muscular well-built small horse

Coggins test—a test for diagnosing equine infectious anemia

colic—a severe digestive disturbance causing pain

colt—male horse under three years of age; if Thoroughbred, under four years of age

combined training—equine sport combining dressage, cross-country jumping, and stadium jumping

condition—a horse's state of health

conformation—the shape of the horse; how he is built

cribbing—a vice in which the horse sets his teeth on an object and sucks in air

cross-bred—a horse whose sire and dam are of different breeds

cutting horse—a horse trained to cut cattle from a herd

dally—to wind the end of the rope around the saddle horn

dam—the mother of a horse

dishing—the horse's foot swinging forward in a sideways arc instead of in a straight line

dressage—a classical system of schooling a horse to become more supple and obedient

easy keeper—a horse that is easy to keep in good flesh

endurance riding—a sport of speed and endurance over distance

eventing—an amateur sport which was formerly a test for cavalry horses (*see Combined Training*)

farrier—a horse shoer

fenders—the wide leather straps from which Western stirrups are suspended

filly—female horse under three years of age; if Thoroughbred, four years of age

floating—filing off the sharp edges of a horse's teeth

foal—a young horse still nursing, of either sex

foaling—giving birth to a foal

founder—*see laminitis*

frog—the vee-shaped growth on the sole of the horse's foot

gallop—a very fast four-beat gait

gelding—a male horse that has been castrated

girth—the band that keeps an English saddle in place

grade horse—one of unknown ancestry

green broke—a horse with very limited training

gymkhana—a collection of games on horseback

halter classes—equine classes judged while handled only from the ground

hands high—height of horse from ground to top of withers, a hand being four inches

hay belly—a belly distended because of eating too much of bulky rations such as hay

horn—the protrusion at the front of a Western saddle

hunting—the pursuit of game while riding

irons—stirrups on an English saddle

jog—a Western slow easy-going two-beat diagonal gait

jogging out—trotting out a horse on a leadline to see if he limps

laminitis—a painful inflammation of the hoof layer directly beneath the hoof wall

laying back—a bad habit of a horse pulling back and trying to break his rope while tied

leathers—on an English saddle, the straps holding the stirrups

lope—a Western slow three-beat combination gait with very little suspension following the third beat

mare—female horse four years or older; in Thoroughbreds five years or older

near side—the left side of the horse

off side—the right side of the horse

osselet—a swelling around the ankle joint caused by an inflammation

paddling—the horse throwing his front feet outward instead of in a straight line as he moves forward

pedigree—a record of a horse's ancestry

performance classes—equine classes judged while ridden

points—black coloration from the knees and hocks down

pole bending—a game involving speed and agility around poles

pommel—the front part of an English or Western saddle

pony—an equine not more than 14.2 hands high

poor keeper—a horse difficult to keep in good flesh

prepotency—the degree to which a parent's qualities are transmitted to its offspring

proud cut—a horse not properly castrated and maintaining much of the behavior of a stallion

purebred—a horse descended from horses of the same breed but not necessarily registered

registered—a horse with papers from a breed association to prove his ancestry

reining horse—a horse trained to perform certain patterns by cues of the reins

ringbone—a bony enlargement of the pastern joint near the coronet

roping horse—a horse trained to aid his rider in roping cattle

running martingale—a strap with rings, running from the girth to the reins which pass through the rings to discourage the horse from carrying his head too high

saddle seat—a style of English riding on specially gaited horses

sidebone—a hardened growth of cartilage directly above and toward the back of the hoof

sire—the father of a horse

soundness—the state of a horse free from injury or flaws

spavins—various types of enlargements in the hock area

splints—abnormal bony growths found on the cannon bone

stallion—a male horse four years old or more; in Thoroughbreds, five years old or more

standing martingale—a strap from the cinch to the bridle's noseband to prevent a horse from throwing his head

steeplechase—a horse race across country over jumps

stirrups—the device on which the rider's feet rest while she is in the saddle

stock horse—(out West) a horse used in working cattle

stud—a stallion used for breeding

tack—horse clothing and equipment for riding and driving

tacked up—horse prepared for riding

thoroughpin—a puffy condition by the hock

throatlatch—the part of the horse underneath the head where the neck begins

throatlatch—the part of the bridle which fastens around the horse's throatlatch, or, jaw strap

tie-down—*see standing martingale*

trail horse—a horse trained to go quietly through or over obstacles usually found on the trail

trot—an English two-beat diagonal gait

twitch—a device put around a horse's upper lip to make him stand still

unsoundness—an abnormality that affects the serviceability of the horse

vaulting—gymnastics on a moving horse

vice—a bad habit exhibited by a horse

walk—a four-beat lateral gait

weanling—a young horse that is weaned

wind puff—a fluid enlargement above the pastern joints

wind sucking—*see cribbing*

winging—throwing the hooves outward as they are picked up

withers—the large bump on top of the horse where the neck joins the back

yearling—a horse between one and two years old

Conformation Of The Horse

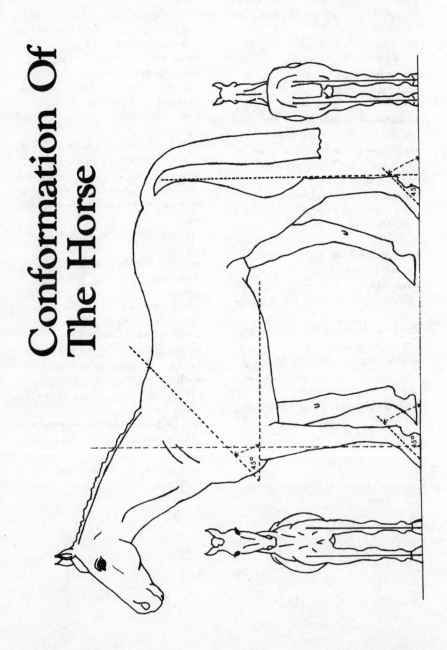

Parts Of The Horse

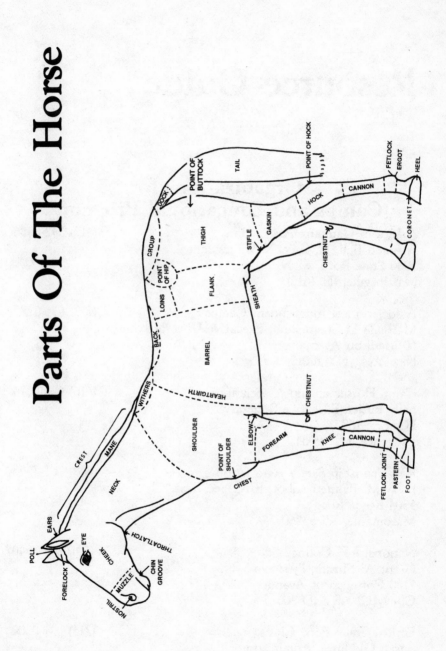

Resource Guide

Organizations for
Camps and Educational Programs

American Camping Association   (317) 342-8456
Armand Ball, Jr., Exec. Vice President
5000 State Road, 67 N
Martinsville, IN 46151

Association of Independent Camps   (212) 679-3230
Mathilde D. Sheinbaum, Executive Director
60 Madison Avenue
New York, NY 10010

Camp Horsemanship Association   (616) 674-8074
Sally Butler, Executive Secretary
P.O. Box 188
Lawrence, MI 49064

Horsemanship Safety Association   (608) 767-2593
Betty M. Bennett-Talbot, Exec. Sec.-Treas.
5304 Reede Road
Mazomanie, WI 53560

National 4-H Council   (301) 961-2940
Grant A. Shrum, President
7100 Connecticut Avenue
Chevy Chase, MD 20815

United States Pony Clubs, Inc.   (215) 436-0300
Susan Giddings, Administrator
893 S. Matlack Street, Suite 110
West Chester, PA 19382-4913

Organizations for
Breeds of Horses and Ponies

Some of these organizations change their addresses from time to time. The Reference Desk of your Public Library should have The Encyclopedia of Associations by Koek and Martin. The index in Volume I, Part 3, gives the reference number of each organization for securing the latest address.

American Crossbred Pony Registry   (201) 875-6399
Lois A. Pellow, Registrar
RD 1, Box 151
Branchville, NJ 07826

American Connemara Pony Society   (203) 491-3521
Elizabeth A. O'Brien, Secretary
P.O. Box 513
Goshen, CT 06756

American Morgan Horse Association   (802) 985-4944
Georgine Winslett, Exec. Director
P.O. Box 960
Shelburne, VT 05482-0960

American Quarter Horse Association   (806) 376-4811
Ronald Blackwell, Exec. Vice President
2701 I-40 E.
Amarillo, TX 79168

American Quarter Pony Association   (515) 675-3669
Linda Grim, Secretary
New Sharon, IA 50207

American Shetland Pony Club   (309) 691-9661
T.R. Huston, Executive Secretary
P.O. Box 3415
Peoria, IL 61614

American Welara Pony Society   (619) 364-2048
John H. Collins, Registrar
P.O. Box 401
Yucca Valley, CA 92284

International Icelandic Pony Association   (805) 688-3869
Elizabeth Haug, Executive Officer
1410 Calzada
Santa Ynez, CA 93460

National Quarter Pony Association   (419) 468-4709
Richard Ekin, President
P.O. Box 955
Galion, OH 44833

Norwegian Fjord Horse Association   (312) 546-7881
Wendalyn Rice, Executive Secretary-Treasurer
24570 W. Chardon Rd.
Grayslake, IL 60030

Pony of the Americas Club, Inc.   (317) 788-0107
Clyde Goff, Executive Secretary
5240 Elmwood Avenue
Indianapolis, IN 46203

Welsh Pony and Cob Society of America   (703) 667-6195
Mrs. Victoria Hedley, Secretary-Treasurer
P.O. Box 2977
Winchester, VA 22601

Horse Magazines

Equus   P.O. Box 57919, Boulder, CO 80322-7919
   A monthly magazine emphasizing care of the horse for all breeds, sports, and riding disciplines.

Chronicle of the Horse   P.O. Box 46, Middleburg, VA 22117
   A weekly magazine with complete coverage of English riding sports including horse showing; it is the official publication for many of those sports.

Dressage & CT   211 West Main St., New London, OH 44851
   A monthly magazine emphasizing education dealing with dressage, Eventing, and the Sport Horse.

Performance Horseman   P.O. Box 927, Farmingdale, NY 11737
   A monthly magazine with instructive articles covering all phases of Western riding, training, and horse care.

Practical Horseman   P.O. Box 927, Farmingdale, NY 11737
 A monthly magazine—the English equivalent of Performance
Horseman by the same publishers, covering riding, training, and horse
care.

Western Horseman   P.O. Box 7980, Colorado Springs, CO 80933
 A monthly magazine devoted to all Western riding, training, sports,
and general horse care.

Organizations for Equestrian Sports

American Horse Shows Association   (212) 972-2472
Adrienne A. Cotter, Exec. Vice President
220 E. 42nd Street
New York, NY 10017

American Endurance Ride Conference   (916) 823-2260
Toni Fonseca, Executive Director
701 High St., Suite 203
Auburn, CA 95603

American Vaulting Association   (408) 867-0402
Judith Bryer, Executive Secretary
20066 Glen Brae Drive
Saratoga, CA 95070

National Cutting Horse Association   (817) 244-6188
Zack T. Wood, Jr., Executive Director
4704 Hwy 377 South
Fort Worth, TX 76116

National Reined Cow Horse Association   (209) 738-8141
Carol Futran, Executive Secretary
5642 West Prospect Drive
Visalia, CA 93291

United States Combined Training Association   (617) 468-7133
Eileen Thomas, Executive Director
292 Bridge Street
South Hamilton, MA 01982-1497

United States Dressage Federation   (402) 474-7632
Lowell Boomer, Executive Secretary
P.O. Box 80668
Lincoln, NE 68501

Recommended Reading And References

The Backyard Horseman
Ron Rude, Mountain Press Publishing Co., Missoula, MT, 1987

This excellent slender book is not only a how-to-ride-Western and how-to-get-along-with-horses book, it establishes a firm foundation for true horsemanship.

Camp Horsemanship Manual (Composite)
Camp Horsemanship Association, Inc., P.O. Box 188, Lawrence, MI 49064

Any child wanting to ride and care for a horse, English or Western, will enjoy reading and learning from this authoritative and cleverly illustrated manual.

The Complete Training of Horse and Rider
Alois Podhajsky, Doubleday and Company, NY, 1963

The classic method of training used at the Spanish Riding School described clearly and logically—Western riders as well as English can benefit.

Guide to Riding and Horse Care
Knox-Thompson and Dickens, Lansdown Press, West Australia, 1985

Beautifully illustrated and written account from "down under" but certainly applicable in the U.S.

The Handbook of Riding
Mary Gordon-Watson, Alfred A. Knopf, Inc., NY, 1982

An excellent guide and reference by a very well-known British expert.

Happy Horsemanship
Dorothy Henderson Pinch, Arco Press, NY, 1966

Written and illustrated for children, this amusing and readable book should help the beginning rider.

Harper's Encyclopedia for Horsemen
Compiled by Louis Taylor, Harper and Row, NY, 1973
All the equine definitions you will probably ever want to know, complete with pictures.

Horse Handbook, Housing and Equipment
Midwest Plan Service, Iowa State University, Ames, IA 50010
Booklet MWPS-15, an excellent reference for proper horse housing, fencing, and gates, from zoning and planning to construction.

A Horse of Your Own
M.A. Stoneridge, Doubleday & Co., Inc., Garden City, NY, 1968
A comprehensive guide for choosing a horse, stabling and nutrition, training, riding, and showing English and Western as well as discussing sports and riding pleasures.

The Horse Owner's Vet Book
Edward C. Straiton, Harper & Row Publishers, Inc., 1979
An authoritative manual on the recognition and treatment of common horse and pony ailments. Every family with a horse will benefit from having this book.

Horses and Horsemanship
M.E. Ensminger, The Interstate Printers and Publishers, Inc., Danville, IL, 1977
A classic textbook in the Animal Agriculture Series for college courses, from stable management and breeding to riding and showing. A very complete reference book.

Invitation to Riding
Sheila Wall Hundt, Simon and Schuster, NY, 1976
This book takes the novice English rider from getting started, up through special skills and various sports, to owning your own horse. Careful and detailed instruction in horsemanship and stable management for adults and older children make this a good book to own.

International Encyclopedia of Horse Breeds
Jane Kidd, HP Books, AZ, 1986
A highly respected British authority produces a beautiful and detailed reference on horse and pony breeds.

The Manual of Horsemanship, 9th Edition
The British Horse Society and the Pony Club, distributed by Half Halt Press, Inc., Middletown, MD, 1988
Written for children, this complete guide to riding and horsemanship is the official text for the Pony Club. Useful also in many ways for Western riders.

The Noble Horse
M. and H. Dossenbach, Portland House, distributed by Crown Publishers, NY, 1987
A beautiful book with lavish illustrations recounting the history of the horse and his relationship with man from the past to the present.

Practical Horseman's Book of Horsekeeping
Edited by M.A. Stoneridge, Doubleday & Company, Inc., Garden City, NY, 1983
A choice selection of articles from past issues of the magazine *Practical Horseman* on the subject of horsekeeping and management.

Practical Western Training, Revised and Enlarged
Dave Jones, 2nd Ed., U. of Oklahoma Press, Norman, OK, 1985
Famous Western trainer explains his successful techniques in riding and training.

The Quarter Horse
Walter D. Osborne, Grosset & Dunlap, NY, 1967
An excellent history of the Quarter Horse and his usefulness from his time of origin until now.

Riding Logic
W. Museler, 5th Ed., Arco Publishing Co., NY, 1984
This classic in English horse literature, updated and illustrated, gives valuable advice on horsemanship to riders of all disciplines.

Small Farms—Livestock Buildings and Equipment
Midwest Plan Service, Iowa State University, Ames, IA 50010
Booklet MWPS-27, a complete guide for rural residents in the designing and building of a small farm from scratch or by adapting existing buildings.

Top Form Book of Horse Care
Frederick Harper, Merck & Company, Inc., NY, 1979
A clear, concise handbook on what you should know about taking care of a horse and why you should know it.

Veterinary Notes for Horse Owners
Capt. M. Horace Hayes, Arco Publishing Co., NY, 1970

A complete reference book for veterinary care, more for the advanced horseman, but a good book to have.

Western Horsemanship
Richard Shrake, ed. by Pat Close, Western Horseman Books, Colorado Springs, CO, 1987

The highly respected Western judge and teacher takes the novice rider from the basics to mid-level riding. Many illustrations.

Index